RYA
Laser
Handbook

Written by Paul Goodison

© RYA Laser Handbook
Copyright RYA 2008
First Published 2008
Reprinted August 2008

The Royal Yachting Association
RYA House, Ensign Way
Hamble, Southampton
Hampshire SO31 4YA

Tel: 0845 345 0400
Fax: 0845 345 0329
E-mail: publications@rya.org.uk
Web: www.rya.org.uk

ISBN 978-1-905104-659 RYA Order Code G53

Acknowledgments

John Emmett for his help with the Laser Radial and 4.7 settings. Pete Cunningham, Nigel Mitchell, Pete Galvin also Chris Gowers and Peter Walker for their help and ideas on health and nutrition.

Photo Credits

Performance Sailcraft, Ocean Images, Tomek Ignatowicz, OnEdition, Getty images.

A CIP record of this book is available from the British Library.
Ring 0845 345 0400 for a free copy of our Publications Catalogue.

Totally Chlorine Free   Sustainable Forests   EMAS VERIFIED ENVIRONMENTAL MANAGEMENT

Published by **The Royal Yachting Association**
RYA House, Ensign Way, Hamble, Southampton SO31 4YA
Tel: 0845 345 0400
Fax: 0845 345 0329
Email: publications@rya.org.uk
Web: www.rya.org.uk

Note: While all reasonable care has been taken in the preparation of this book, the publisher takes no responsibility for the use of the methods or products or contracts described in the book.

Illustrator: Pete Galvin
Cover design: Pete Galvin
Typeset: Batt Creative
Proof-reading and indexing: Alan Thatcher
Printed by: Printed in China through World Print

Contents

Contents

Contents

Contents

Contents

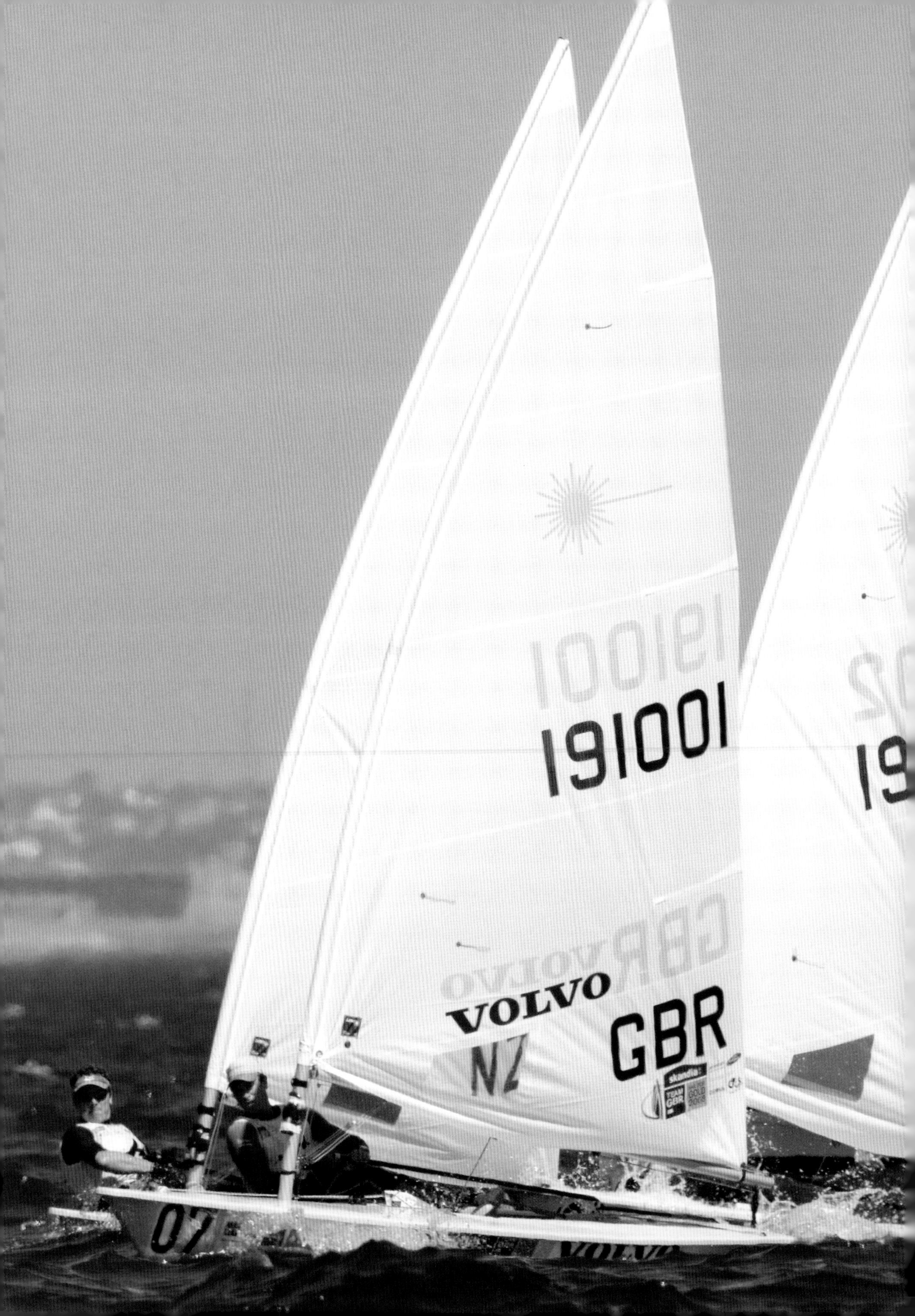
191001
VOLVO
GBR
NZ
07

Foreword

I was delighted when Paul was asked to write a book on the Laser Class. Having been a committed single-handed sailor for much of my active sailing career, and as a former coach, I have been privileged to work with many of the greats of British Laser sailing up until the end of the Sydney Games in 2000 and observed closely most of the overseas legends, such as the Brazilian, Robert Sheidt (7 times winner of the World Championships) and Michael Blackburn (Olympic medalist), but it was clear to me in the build up to Sydney, where Ben Ainslie had asked Paul to act as his "tune up" leading up to the Games, that British Laser sailing was in safe hands moving forwards - and so it has proved. Paul was undoubtedly a vital ingredient in Ben's 2000 Gold medal winning success in Sydney and has since gone on from strength to strength with his own achievements.

Paul is one of those apparently laid back characters, who seems to get phased by very little - which belies his true Northern (Yorkshire) grit. No-one has so consistently medaled at recent Laser World championships, coming back time and time again from positions no-one has a right to expect a medal from!

It is his understated self belief (as well as an acidic dry sense of humour) that makes him such a compelling and engaging character, who puts so much back into the sport - and still turns out top performances at home and in International events alike.

Most of racing a Laser is about being beaten - and dealing with it - temperament is hugely important - and Paul has demonstrated his, time and time again.

You can only get better from reading this book.

John Derbyshire
RYA Manager/ Performance Director

Introduction

When I started sailing I learnt mainly whilst crewing for my father, but was always desperate to helm. As I became more confident, my Dad, a keen racing helmsman, was being pushed more and more to the front of the boat by my eagerness to helm! Eventually I started sailing Toppers and helming a National 12. Although I loved sailing with others it soon became evident that I was more suited to single-handed sailing – I wanted out and out control. After sailing a few classes including Toppers, Streakers and Splashes, I convinced my parents to buy a Laser and it soon became clear that it was the class for me. There was organised training, a youth squad and large fleets with great competitions all over the country. The boats were simple and equal so the competition was on a level playing field – nobody had a faster boat or sails. At the end of the day it was the guy who was sailing the boat the best that was winning the races and I liked that there were no excuses although I'm sure I've made a few in my time.

When I first started Laser sailing I couldn't believe how fast the top sailors could make their boats go especially when sailing in waves. I watched them as much as possible when racing to see what they were doing; I probably should have been concentrating on what I was doing a little more. I can remember looking through pictures in magazines in great detail trying to work out what they were doing differently and how I could improve. I was really lucky to be the youngest sailor in a development squad including Ben Ainslie, Iain Percy, Andrew Simpson and Hugh Styles who are all amazing sailors in their own right. I learnt so much about sailing with this group, there was great respect and a real hunger to win, and the competitive spirit raised everyones' performance.

A great opportunity arose when, before the Sydney Olympics, I was Ben's training partner and the rivalry really brought out the best in our performances. It was the same when I teamed up with Mark Howard prior to the Athens Olympics. By sharing thoughts and having an open mind you can challenge each other and lift your sailing to the next level.

My hope is that you will be able to use this book to answer your questions and help fast track your learning. I have tried to use detailed pictures and clear illustrations to demonstrate techniques and my thoughts. I hope that this book will help facilitate your learning and introduce you to new skills and ways of thinking to improve your sailing.

Most of all enjoy your time on the water in this amazing sport.

Paul Goodison

1 The Laser

Sailing a Laser is often thought to be one of the purest forms of sailing. With the Laser's simple set up it is a great way to get on the water whether you want a peaceful cruise or an Olympic challenge. The option of the three rigs, 4.7, Radial and Standard means that whatever your shape, size or skill level there is always a boat which will suit you. As a one-design class there are only very small differences between boats, making racing very tight. It's the best sailor that wins not the one with the best designed equipment.

The new controls, combined with the various rigs have opened the Laser up to a wider range of weight and ages. The 4.7 is a great starter boat for junior and smaller sailors; the Radial, ideal for youth sailors and now the women's Olympic single hander; and the Standard rig is one of the most competitive fleets in the world for senior sailors.

18610

VOLVO

GB

TEAM
VOLVO

uk sport
LOTTERY FUNDED

1 The Laser

Getting started

There are thousands of Lasers around the world and a cheap way to get started is to buy a second-hand boat and, depending on your budget there is a vast choice. Although there is always an element of 'you get what you pay for' and by paying attention to a few key areas a second-hand boat can be as good a buy and as competitive as a new one.

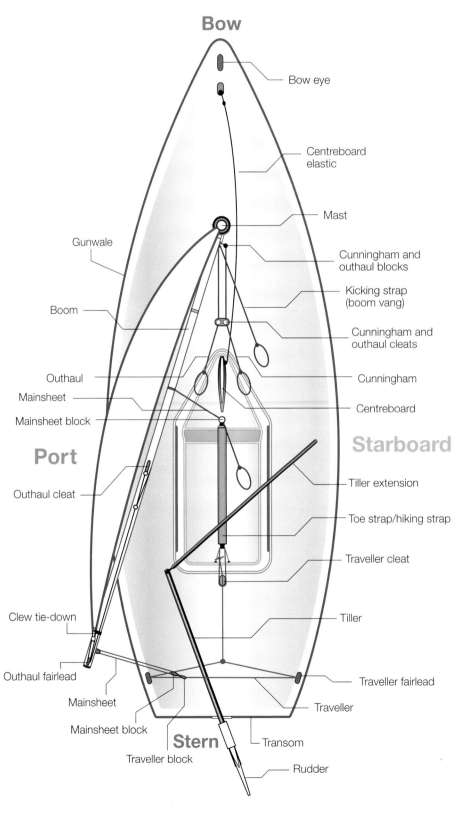

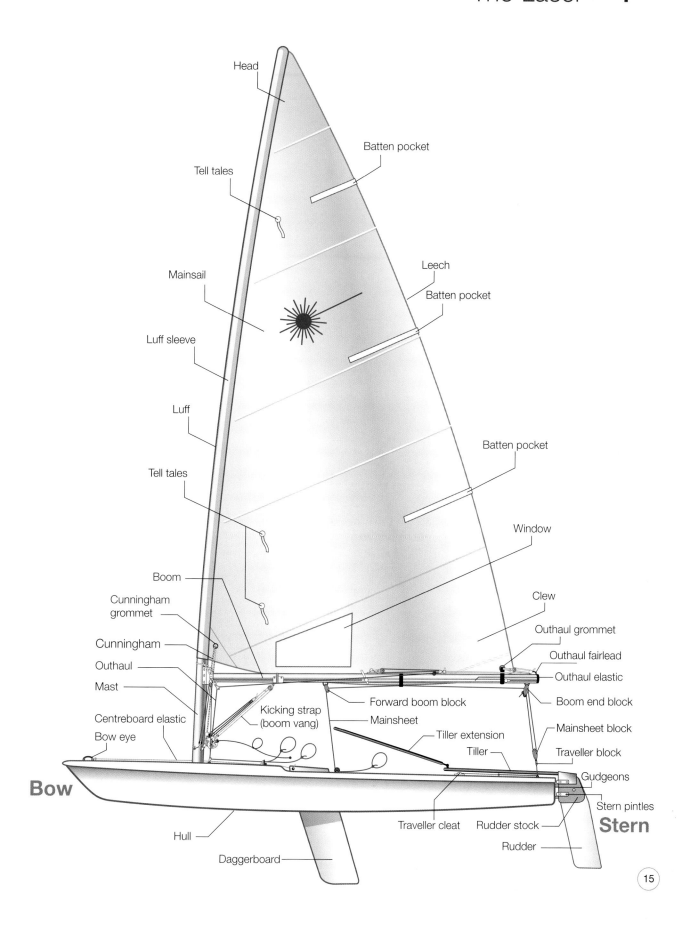

Head

Batten pocket

Tell tales

Leech

Batten pocket

Mainsail

Luff sleeve

Luff

Tell tales

Batten pocket

Window

Boom

Clew

Cunningham grommet

Outhaul grommet

Cunningham

Outhaul fairlead

Outhaul

Outhaul elastic

Mast

Forward boom block

Boom end block

Centreboard elastic

Kicking strap (boom vang)

Mainsheet

Mainsheet block

Bow eye

Tiller extension

Traveller block

Tiller

Gudgeons

Bow

Stern pintles

Stern

Hull

Traveller cleat

Rudder stock

Daggerboard

Rudder

1 The Laser

What to look for when buying a used boat

The Hull
Ideally the hull should be smooth underneath, if there are a few scratches don't be put off, but the fewer the better. Look carefully around the underside of the mast step and the daggerboard case for signs of any stress cracks. This will give a good indication of how much use the boat has had. In older boats these cracks are quite common and are not always a serious problem. Superficial cracks can be lightly sanded and then polished out; if they are deep they will need to be filled.

In older boats the alignment of the rudder and the daggerboard will need checking. Turn the boat upside down with the foils in place; looking along the length of the boat, the rudder and daggerboard should be vertical with the trailing edges aligned.

Carefully look at the underside for any cracks or imperfections

Deck fittings
Check that the deck fitting screws are tight. If the screws spin and fail to bite there is a potential problem, especially if water has got into the wooden backing blocks underneath the fittings. If there is any wood rot the area will need to be dried out, filled with epoxy and re-drilled to resolve the problem.

Spars
The spars should be straight, look down the sections or place them parallel to each other to check this. The rivets holding the fittings may become loose, this is no real problem as the fittings can be re-riveted. Check for any cracks on the fittings as this is where the mast will fail.

Foils
The foils should be free from any cracks, so check the rudder where the tie down line passes through because this is where the rudder may break if cracked.

Sail and Lines
Look at the sail and the lines to see if they will need replacing in the near future. The older the sail the softer the cloth will feel to the touch, newer sails feel more crispy and will perform much better. Worn ropes are easily and relatively cheap to replace.

Getting the most out of your boat

Sail

Sails are best kept rolled around a pole or the top mast to prevent creasing and damage. The batten pockets have elastic sewn into the front of them to tension the battens against the leech. The battens can miss the elastic so it is important to check that they are located properly before you go out on the water.

Battens

The batten ends may get stuck behind the elastic in the batten pockets and can be really difficult to remove. To prevent this happening tape the ends on or remove the ends and epoxy or glue them back on to the batten.

Tell tales

The best position for tell tales is just above the window and one at the halfway point between the luff and top batten. Don't put them too close to the mast because the airflow is too disturbed and if they are too far back they are less sensitive. See photo below.

Wind indicators

This is down to personal preference. A Windex on the top of the mast gives a better reading of the wind, while a Windex on the bow of the boat or around the mast just below the boom will be easier to see while looking at the waves in front of the bow whilst sailing.

Battens

Wind indicator on the bow

Tell tales at work

1   The Laser

Spars

The spars need to be regularly checked to ensure that they are straight. It is normal for the top mast to become slightly bent while sailing, especially with high kicker tensions in windy weather.

The easiest way to straighten out the top mast is by placing it in the bottom mast and resting one end on a solid surface and the other on the floor. Rotate the mast so the outside of the bend is facing up and apply a smooth downward pressure, stopping regularly to look down the mast and checking if the mast is straightening (see photo 3).

If you have to regularly straighten the mast, if it appears to be bending more each time or it bends when less kicker pressure is applied then the mast needs to be changed.

This may require buying a new mast or doing an "end for end" on the current one.

"End for end"

To "end for end" a top mast:

Straighten the mast (as previously described).

Drill the rivets out so the mast collars and plugs can be removed. Be careful not to damage the fittings as they can be reused (see photo 1).

Slide the collars onto the new ends, measure the distance between the collar and bottom of the mast 305mm+ or - and mark with a marker pen (see photo 2).

With the collars in place drill new holes through the plastic and into the mast and re-rivet the fittings in place.

Place rivets into the empty holes where the old fittings used to be to make the mast watertight.

Remove the mast fittings

Place the plugs on the new end and mark before drilling

Apply direct pressure against the bend

Rudder and daggerboard

The rudderstock needs to be checked regularly for signs of cracking around the pintles. If the rivets around the pintles are loose this will cause slop in the tiller when steering. The standard bolt should be replaced with the maximum legal size which is 9.5mm diameter with a 20mm diameter washer. Have this bolt as tight as possible to get a precise solid feel on the tiller. The foils should have a straight trailing edge and be smooth.

Gudgeons

Play in the steering and rudder often originates from the gudgeons. The screws need to be as tight as possible without being over tightened - too tight and it will bend the plastic causing the gudgeons to flex. If the boat is used regularly the gudgeons should be replaced every season, you can prolong their life by turning them upside down once they show signs of wearing.

Tiller and extension

There are several makes and models available and which to choose is mainly down to personal preference and budget. The key area to look for in a tiller is the fit in the stock and its stiffness; this is critical because a sloppy fitting or bendy tiller will reduce the feel and therefore the feedback while sailing. The tiller needs to be as low to the deck as possible to reduce the height of the traveller, but high enough so that it doesn't touch the traveller cleat when a slight pressure is applied. It's important to have a low traveller so that the mainsheet blocks stay in the corner of the transom when sailing upwind.

The tiller extension is again down to personal preference. The longer the tiller extension the easier it is to steer while fully hiked or sitting forward, however it does make tacking, gybing and general boat handling more difficult. A good length can be seen in the picture below. The tiller is in the stock and tiller and extension are straight. The end of the extension goes just past the daggerboard stop when the board is fully down.

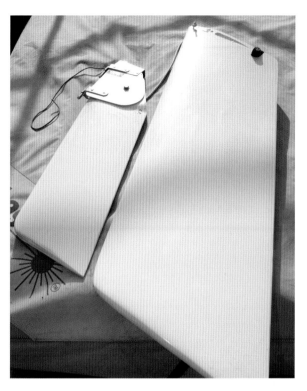

ACME American tiller

The ideal tiller extension length

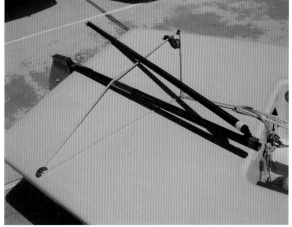

Marstrom tiller

1 The Laser

Leaking hulls

It is not uncommon for a hull to develop a leak. The best way to check for leaks is to tape over the breathe-hole which is located under the toe strap. Blow into the bunghole or use an air line to pressurise the hull, quickly inserting the bung to stop the air from escaping. Drip soapy water on to and around all the deck fittings, watching for any bubbles to appear. Key fittings to check first are the mainsheet block and friction pad because water is thrust up here when planing or being towed.

Other areas to check are the self-bailer ring, gudgeons, and the hull/deck joint in the daggerboard case. Most leaks can be easily fixed by using a silicone sealant or something similar. A leak in the daggerboard case will require the use of marine filler, as silicone sealant will rub off as the board is pushed up and down.

Key things to remember when rigging the boat

Remember to put the bung in.

Make sure the rivet on the top mast is aligned with the gooseneck.

Make sure the sail is square on the mast top and aligned with the gooseneck (see picture below).

Remove any debris from the mast foot before putting it in the mast step.

Make sure all knots and split pins are secure.

Thread mainsheet, remembering the boom eye and knot both ends of the mainsheet.

Lasers are delivered from the manufacturer ready to sail, but if you want to get the best performance out of your new boat it is worth taking some time on the final preparations (see Regatta Boat Preparation page 126).

Align the top of the sail with the gooseneck by looking down the mast

2 Standard Control Lines

Manufacturers sell the Laser with various specifications from standard to race prepared. If you have a standard package, new or old, and don't want to upgrade to the new controls there are several ways of making life easier. By using smooth rope with blocks or metal thimbles at turning points the friction can be greatly reduced. The best way to tie the ropes is shown below in the illustrations.

If you are thinking of racing more seriously, then it is a good idea to upgrade to the new control system. You can purchase the fittings individually or buy a pre-pack such as the Laser GXD system. The pack comes with all the blocks needed, with the ropes cut to length. The first thing to upgrade would be the outhaul and Cunningham as this will make the biggest difference to the boat.

Cunningham

This system is a 6:1 system very similar to the new GXD system but only using 1 rope. If the bowlines have metal thimbles inserted in them or are replaced by blocks the system is more efficient. A 4mm rope should be used.

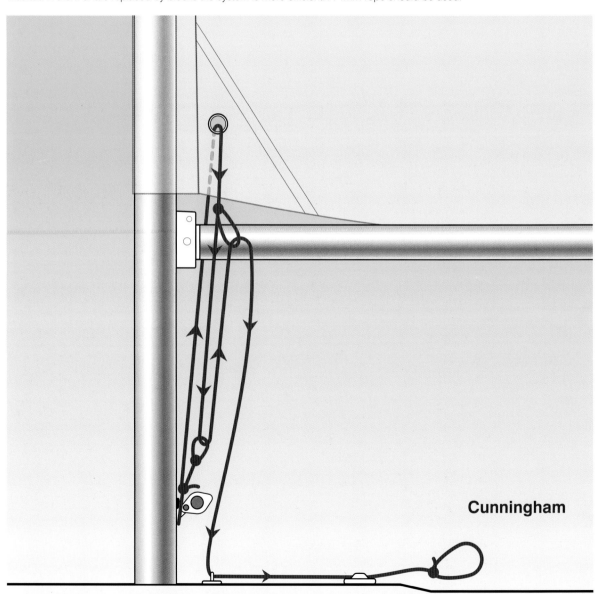

Cunningham

Outhaul

This 9:1 system allows a more accurate adjustment of the outhaul. Again, if metal thimbles are used in the bowlines or blocks are used the system is much more efficient. A 4mm rope should be used.

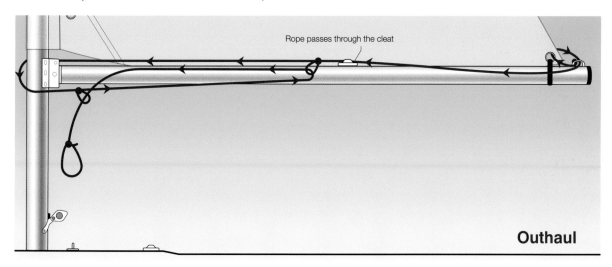

Rope passes through the cleat

Outhaul

Kicker

The Kicker uses an 8:1 system which seems to be the best compromise between purchase and range. When a block or a metal thimble is used in the bowline the system is much more efficient. Best to use a 5mm rope.

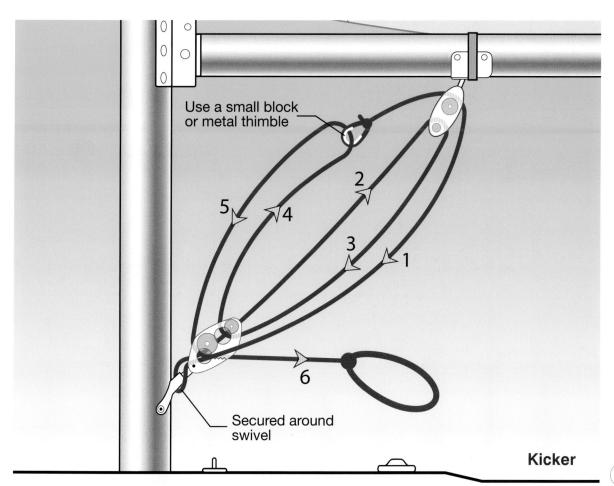

Use a small block or metal thimble

Secured around swivel

Kicker

3   The New Control Lines

New controls have made the Laser much easier to sail than in the past. The use of blocks and deck lead cleats make sail adjustment more precise and easier. There are several different variations of how to set the new systems up but I have found the following the best compromise for sail adjustment with enough purchase to make life easier without the excess rope created by large purchase systems. The photographs and illustrations will help guide you through tying the knots in the right place and threading the ropes the correct way.

Kicker 9-1 system

What's needed?

- 1.4m - 3mm cream coloured rope
- 3.5m - 4mm red rope

- 1x Harken kicker base
- 1x 16mm double air block with becket
- 1x Holt Allen HA-4479 + washers, bolt and key, 40cm tube for the handle

1. With the boat rigged, place the top block onto the boom and secure with tape or a piece of elastic.See illustration on page 27. Then attach the Harken kicker base into the kicker tang.

2. Tie the cream rope to the top block and then thread the rope through the vertical block on the main fitting and back through the top block.

3. Next tie the double air block to the line so the blocks sit next to the top blocks when the kicker is fully released. There should be a little bit of slack when the sail is holding the boom up.

4. Thread the red rope through the cleat and around the internal block on the main fitting. Next thread the red rope through the double air block at the boom, and back through the horizontal blocks and tie the rope using a bowline around the remaining roller on the double air block.

5. Feed a 40cm piece of tube over the excess rope at the cleat and tie a bowline to secure the tube as a handle. The handle should be close to the cleat in the maximum off position.

Tie the tail of the remaining rope (about a metre) to the daggerboard eye.

If you find it difficult to apply enough tension with the 9:1 system use all the purchase to make the kicker a more powerful 16:1 system. The downside of this system is that there is more rope to get tangled up when the kicker is fully on. When sheeting block to block the kicker key can occasionally drop out so it's a good idea to tie a piece of elastic or electricians' tape around the boom to secure the kicker key.

The blocks should be in this position when fully eased.

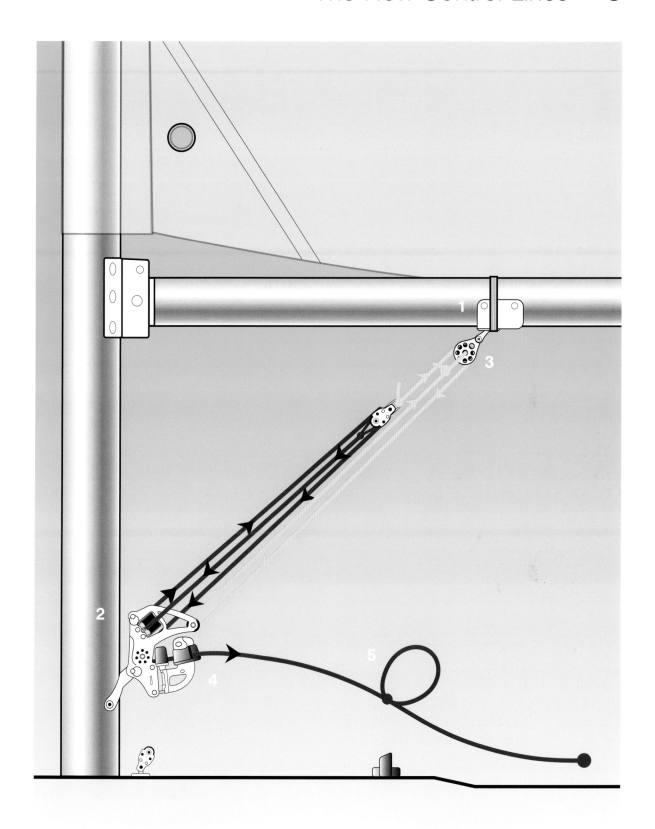

3 The New Control Lines

Cunningham 6-1 system

What's needed?

- 1.3m - 5mm white rope
- 3m - 4mm blue rope
- 0.5m - 3mm light blue rope
- 1x 16mm air block
- 1x 16mm air block with becket

1. Using the light blue rope tie a block around the mast below the kicker tang.

2. Now take the white rope and tie one end to the block with a becket then pass the rope through the Cunningham's eye (on the sail) and tie around the kicker tang using a bowline. Tie the rope so that the top block sits just below the gooseneck when slack.

3. Using the blue rope tie one end to the becket on the top block and then thread it through the block tied at the kicker tang and back up through the top block, and then down to the deck block and back to the cleat. Use a bowline for the handle and position this so it is next to the cleat when Cunningham is slack.

Cut off any excess of rope.

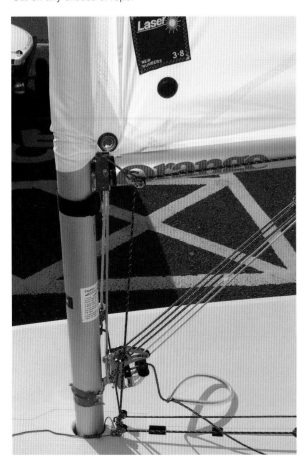

Cunningham 6.1 system

For lighter sailors or anyone using a very old sail: it is essential to put the Cunningham on one side of the sail in strong winds, this allows the sail to be pulled down one side of the boom allowing the tension to be increased (see photo 2).

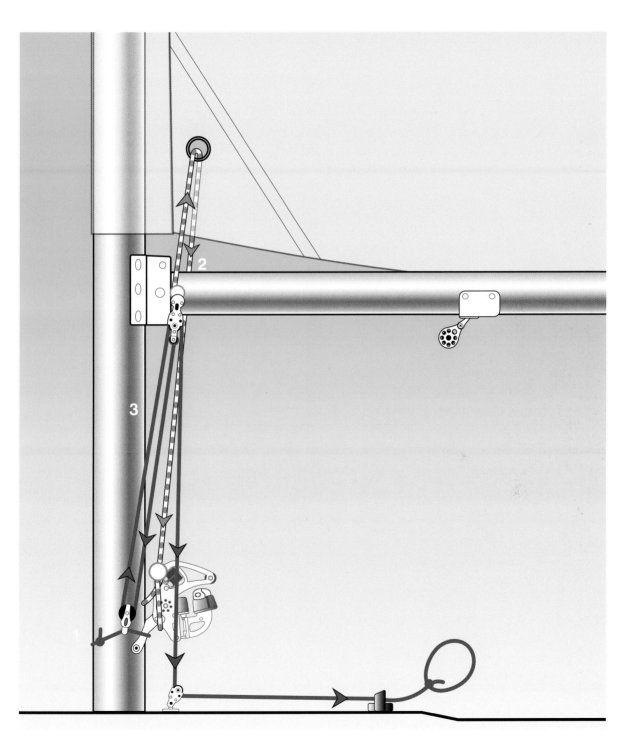

You can also opt for either a 3-1 or 6-1 system. I used to use the 3-1 because I didn't like the idea of the extra rope in the cockpit; however the 6-1 system allows much more accurate adjustment of the sail.

3   The New Control Lines

Outhaul

What's needed?

- 0.2m - 3mm pink rope
- 0.2m - 3mm blue rope
- 0.5m - 3mm white rope
- 1.5m - 4mm white rope
- 4m - 4mm red rope
- 1.5m - 6mm elastic + outhaul strap
- 3x 16mm air block
- 1x 16mm air block with becket

1. With the short white rope tie a bowline around the mast above the gooseneck then using the tail of the rope attach an air block using a bowline.

2. Using the pink rope attach an air block to the clew of the sail.

3. With the blue rope attach an air block to the outhaul cleat in the middle of the boom.

4. Tie the red rope to the becket of the air block and also the remaining white rope to the end of this block. (4)

5. Thread the red rope through the block which is tied onto the boom cleat, then take it back through itself. Pull the blocks apart 12 inches/30cm and tie a stopper knot to prevent the blocks releasing anymore than this. Thread the tail through the block which is attached at the boom down to the deck and back to the cleat (see photo 2).

   Attach the clew Velcro strap through the clew of the sail and the boom and tightly fasten.

6. With the white rope attached to the air block with becket, thread the tail through the boom eye around the clew block on the sail and back to the boom eye and tie here.

7. Thread the elastic through the clew strap and tie a stopper knot. Pull the opposite end to the boom cleat and tie around the boom, the elastic should be heavily tensioned (see photos 2 & 3).

Boom end

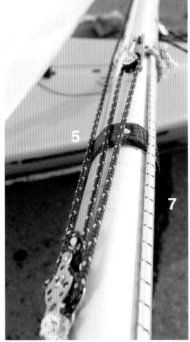

Boom Purchase System

Note the Cunningham rope is outside rope

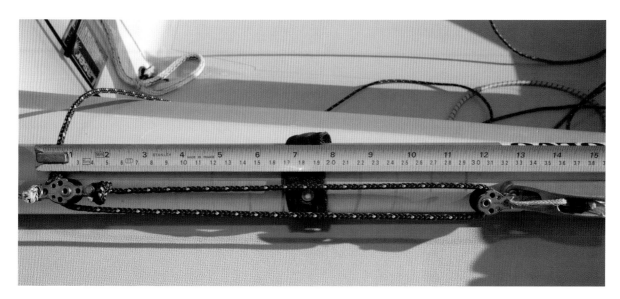

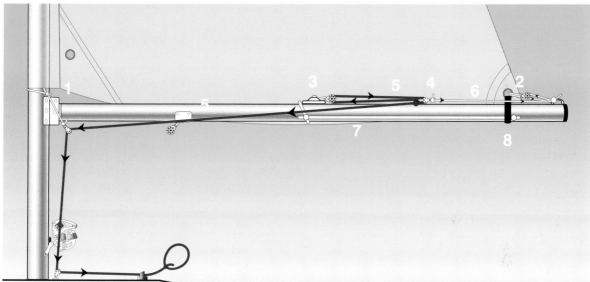

There are a number of ways to rig the outhaul and I have found that the 9-1 system allows more accurate adjustment and rigged in the following way with calibration on the boom makes it easy to repeat settings. The new Velcro straps have also increased the efficiency of the outhaul as the strap slides easily along the boom. It is important to replace the strap as soon as the Velcro starts to lose its grip strength, a worn strap may come undone while sailing. There is also the option to use a new metal fitting, this is a great alternative to a strap.

The elastic strop helps the outhaul to be released in lighter winds (8) and is very efficient when the elastic is passed through the Velcro strap as indicated. If the elastic is threaded through the sail eye the foot of the sail can be disturbed.

3 The New Control Lines

Toe Strap

There are several types of toe straps available and which to use is down to personal preference. Toe straps need to be comfortable and allow the pressure to spread across the feet. The strap should be rigid enough to prevent twist, making sure it is comfortable out of tacks and gybes. Use a length of elastic to stop the toe strap sagging. An adjustable toe strap is essential for racing as we need different lengths on different legs of the course.

To do this we need:

1m - 5mm white rope   1.8m - 5mm elastic

Tie a small bowline around the starboard eye. Pass the rope through the toe strap, through the port eye and then back through both the bowline and the starboard eye. Pass the elastic through the toe strap and back around the traveller cleat under the traveller rope. Pull tight and tie together using a reef knot.

Adjustable toe strap system

Adjusting the toe strap while sailing

Rudder Tie Down

The rudder tie needs to be really tight to hold the rudder down and to secure the tiller into the stock. To do this push the rudder fully down and the tiller right into the stock. Pull the tie down rope tight and make a loop in the rope where it exits the stock.

1. Pass the rope around the tiller point and back through the loop.

2. Pull the rope as tight as possible and then secure by passing the rope around itself and pulling through.

3. Done this way the rope can easily be released by one pull. Tidy up the remaining rope by wrapping it back around itself.

1

2

3

Traveller

Rope - use 3m of 5mm Vectran. To do this we need to pass the rope through the deck fairlead, through the traveller blocks and then through the other fairlead. Use a bowline to tie the rope together to create a small triangle.

1. Pass the tail through the cleat creating a small handle.

2. Tying the traveller using a single bowline helps to reduce the height of the knot. The smaller the triangle created when the rope is tied the easier it will be to gain greater tension.

3. The rope should have minimal stretch.

The mast retainer helps to prevent the elastic getting caught on the kicker fitting when the board is raised.

Control Handles

To be able to apply the right amount of pressure it is important to have a good handle.

1. I use a rubber tube to make the kicker handle more comfortable and a simple bowline for the outhaul and Cunningham.

2. A rubber tube may also be used here if desired. This reduces the amount of rope needed: cut off any excess as it is not needed and will only get in the way.

3. To stop the kicker handle falling in the water tie with the tail of the rope to the daggerboard.

Goodies Tip

- The mainsheet blocks need to be heavily taped to stop them from twisting and jamming while sailing.

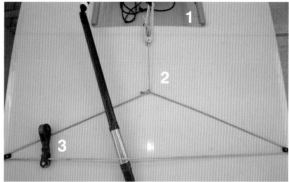

Block taped to prevent twisting

Daggerboard Elastic

The daggerboard elastic helps to keep the board up or down while sailing. It is critical to get the right tension on the elastic - too tight and it is difficult to adjust - too loose and the board slips while sailing. I like to tie a loop in the mast retaining line and thread the elastic through it (1). This stops the elastic from getting tangled around the kicker fitting when manoeuvring with the board raised. Use a simple stopper knot through the daggerboard to secure the elastic - this keeps the control lines from being snagged. A hook on the bow at the other end makes it easier to remove.

Mainsheet

The mainsheet needs to be as thin as you can comfortably handle, the thinner the rope the easier it will run through the blocks but if it is too thin it will be difficult to hold and uncomfortable. I think a 6mm diameter rope is about right but some sailors choose to use rope as thin as 5mm diameter in light winds. It is also important to have the correct length so that the boom can't go too far beyond 90 degrees. Too much rope will lead to a mess in the cockpit and the rope getting tangled. Make sure the ratchet block is well sprung and holds the block vertical.

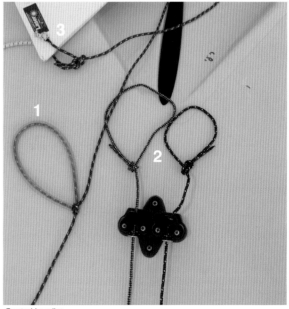

Control handles

3   The New Control Lines

A Quick Guide To New Rope Dimensions

Try to use ropes of different colours to avoid confusion

Rope	Length	Diameter	Material
Mainsheet	12.5m	6mm	Spectra®
Traveller	3m	5mm	Vectran®
Toe strap	1m	5mm	
	1.8m	5mm	Elastic
Daggerboard	2m	5mm	Elastic
Cunningham	1.3m	5mm	Vectran®
	3m	4mm	
	0.5m	3mm	
	1x	16mm air block	
	1x	16mm air block with becket	
Outhaul	0.3m	3mm	
	0.5m	3mm	
	1.5m	4mm	
	4m	4mm	
	1.5m	6mm	Elastic + outhaul strap
	3x	16mm air block	
	1x	16mm air block with becket	
Kicker	1.4m	3mm	Vectran®
	3.5m	4mm	
	1x	Harken kicker base	
	1x	16mm double air block with becket	
	1x	Holt Allen HA-4479 + washers, bolt and key	
Mast retainer	1m	3mm	

4 Basic sail controls and their effects

A Laser sail is fairly basic in design and material which allows the shape to be easily changed by using the control lines. To set the sail you need to understand how each control will affect the rig.

Kicker

The kicker (also referred to as the vang), is a way of controlling the leech tension of the sail and the mast bend. In downwind sailing more kicker means more leech tension and more mast bends, creating a flatter sail with less twist. Less kicker gives a fuller sail and more twist. When the kicker is tightened the boom is pushed into the mast causing it to bend and the leech is also tightened as the end of the boom is moved vertically down. When sailing upwind this is slightly different as the mainsheet has greater control over the leech tension and does this without forcing the mast to bend low down. The kicker is also used upwind to bend the mast and de-power the sail.

Cunningham

The Cunningham controls and tensions the front (luff) of the sail. When pulled tight this makes the luff tension closer to the tension of the leech, so making the leech relatively less tight and more prone to open. The Cunningham also pulls the centre of effort forward in the sail.

Outhaul

This controls the camber or depth of the sail lower down in the rig. The deeper the outhaul the more lift the sail produces providing power, however as the lift (power) increases so does the drag. For each point of sailing there is an optimum, it is always a trade between the amount of power for a given amount of drag. So we have to come to a compromise.

Clew tie

This control only has one setting and holds the clew of the sail down to the boom and should be tight enough to prevent the clew rising more than 5mm from the boom.

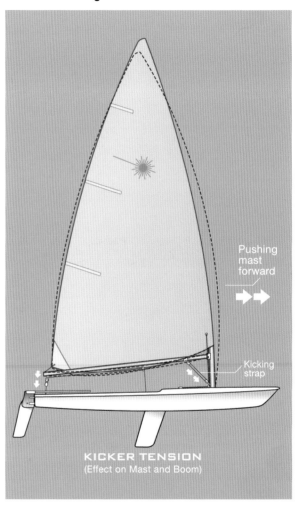

Pushing mast forward

Kicking strap

KICKER TENSION
(Effect on Mast and Boom)

Mainsheet

Controls how far the sail can be sheeted and eased. It needs to be long enough to allow the boom to go just beyond 90 degrees. The tail end can be tied to the toe strap to help prevent knots. It is a good idea to make a mark on the mainsheet to identify when the boom is at 90 degrees for use as a reference point.

If you have a good understanding of the sail controls then it is possible to optimise the shape of the sail for different wind and wave conditions.

Traveller

When sailing upwind the traveller controls the sheeting angle of the sail. The traveller needs to be tight to hold the blocks in the corner of the stern when the mainsheet is sheeted in (1). If the traveller is too tight this holds the tiller straight and could reduce the feel on the tiller - the pressure you feel on the tiller is how much force is needed. If the traveller is too tight it holds the tiller straight reducing the feel. If the traveller is loose then the blocks will rise into the middle of the boat creating a narrower sheeting angle making the leech of the sail more hooked and less efficient creating drag (2). The traveller very rarely needs to be adjusted and is always pulled tight in all but the lightest winds.

Tight traveller blocks in corner

Loose traveller blocks have risen towards centre line causing a hooked exit

4   Basic sail controls and their effects

Advanced Sail Setting Theory

The Sail

The sail comes from the manufacturer with a set shape; this shape is induced into the sail through the seams and the luff curve when the sail is put together. Sail cloth is very soft and flexible so the set shape induced by the sail maker changes greatly in differing wind strengths. The two-piece flexible mast emphasises this change as the mast bends, increasing and decreasing luff curve. The sail shape therefore changes all the time so you will need to adjust the controls regularly to maintain the optimum shape.

The biggest problems in sail setting usually occur when the wind is strong and you are using an older sail. Because the sail cloth is soft the draft of the sail (the area of most fullness) moves back when the pressure in the sail increases. If insufficient Cunningham is used this becomes too far back, resulting in an increased amount of weather helm being created.

Spar stiffness

The set distance between the upper mast collars is 305mm with a tolerance of +/- 5mm. If the minimum distance of 300mm is used the mast will be slightly longer with less top mast in the bottom section, effectively making the mast softer and more bendy. If the maximum distance of 310mm is used there is more of the top mast in the bottom mast and the section will be stiffer but shorter. It is generally agreed that to maximise boat speed heavier sailors require stiffer rigs and lighter sailors need softer rigs.

Distance between upper mast collars 305mm + or - 5mm

Check the sail to see the effect of the controls on the sail

5   Basic Manoeuvres

Sheeting

It is important to use a double-handed technique when sheeting. The mainsheet should be pulled in using a hand over hand technique. Grab the sheet at the block with the front hand and pull towards the shoulder using the other hand then holding the tiller grab the mainsheet again close to the block and pull towards the chest and repeat.

Tacking

Tacking is when the bow of the boat passes through the wind. When racing it is usual only to tack from a close hauled course to a close hauled course, so this is what we now focus on. Tacking is one of the most used manoeuvres in sailing and one where large gains can be made. The difference between a good and a bad tack can result in a gain or loss of a boat length in distance. When racing we can expect to do ten tacks per beat, if we can make these good we can potentially gain ten boat lengths in the beat alone. Tacking is therefore an essential skill to master.

Differing sea states and wind strengths will require different tacking techniques; the two extremes of these are outlined in illustrations 1 and 2.

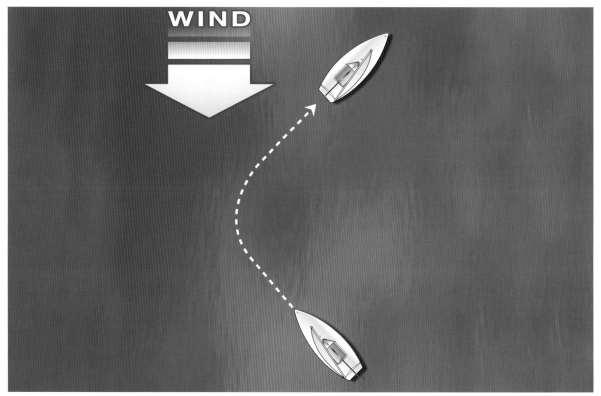

Illustration 1: Light wind tack track through the water

See Training Exercise 6

Light Wind Tack

In lighter winds and flatter water the boat is able to hold speed through the tacks easier as there is minimal resistance from waves and wind. In these tacks a smaller tiller/rudder angle is required so the momentum can be maintained. A long arc is preferred as the track through the water (see illustration 1). Using a smaller tiller angle (pushing the tiller end no further than halfway between the edge of the cockpit and the gunwale) and rolling the boat means that the rudder will stop the boat slowing down as much and the boat will turn slower helping to create a longer arc through the water. In theory this will help gain distance to windward and therefore reduce the distance to the mark. Check the track through the water by looking at the bubbles and water after the tack to see how you have done. The key to light tacks is to be smooth in tiller and body movement.

Illustration 2: Stronger winds require a tighter turn in the tack

Strong Wind Tack

As the wind and sea builds it is much more difficult to maintain the speed through the turn due to the resistance of the waves and wind. In strong winds the tack therefore needs to be much faster and the track through the water is a tighter arc, this gets the boat onto the new tack as soon as possible. The speed of the tack is increased by pushing the tiller further creating a larger rudder angle; we also need to exit the tack lower than a close hauled course enabling the boat to accelerate back up to speed faster. If we come out of the tack on or above a close hauled course the boat speed will be slow, reducing the efficiency of the foils, the result being the boat slips a little sideways when trying to accelerate. The key to a good heavy wind tack is getting the boat back up to speed on the new tack by crossing the boat quickly and hiking extra hard out of the tack to bring the boat flat.

5 Basic Manoeuvres

Normal Tack

Tacking quick guide

Sail on a close-hauled course.

Check to windward and over your front shoulder that it is clear to tack.

Check that there is not going to be any sudden change in wind or wave conditions before entering the tack.

Pick a flatter smoother patch of water.

Slowly push the tiller away.

As the boat starts to heel to windward, place the back foot over the toe strap.

As the bow goes through head to wind start to move the body inboard.

Pass under the boom smoothly easing the mainsheet slightly.

As the boat comes down to a close-hauled course. move smoothly out to the new side.

Allow the boat to heel slightly to leeward before straightening the tiller and hiking out on the new tack while sheeting back in.

When settled pass the mainsheet hand to the tiller and change hands.

Kicker tension is important for the acceleration out of tacks. The kicker will help to keep the leech tight and this helps the boat accelerate when it is pulled flat. A good tack is when you lose very little speed during the manoeuvre, and in lighter winds gain a little extra.

The key differences between a normal tack and heavy wind tack (see p 46) is the speed of transition. The boat needs to be turned faster and the body will need to move faster to keep up. Push the tiller further than before, to the edge of the gunwale (5). This will speed up the turn. The body also needs to move earlier and faster as the boat doesn't need to be rolled. Start to cross the boat before it passes head to wind (4) and aim to go straight out hiking at the new side (7) to pull the boat flat. Leave the mainsheet eased slightly until the boat is back up to speed.

Check to windward and look for a flat spot in the waves

Slowly steer into the turn

Lift the back foot over the toe strap

As the boat passes head to wind start to lean into the boat

Reach across with your back hand & pull mainsheet tauht with the front hand

Straighten the tiller as you cross the boat

Jump straight out under the toe strap to pull the boat flat

Pull the mainsheet across to tiller hand

Change hands

Sail away

5 Basic Manoeuvres

Heavy Wind Tack

The key difference between a normal tack and a heavy wind tack is the speed of transition. The boat needs to be turned faster and the body will need to move faster to keep up. Push the tiller further than before, to the edge on the gunwale (5). This will speed up the turn. The body also needs to move earlier and faster as the boat doesn't need to be rolled. Start to cross the boat before it passes head to wind (4) and aim to go straight out hiking at the new side (7) to pull the boat flat. Leave the mainsheet eased sightly until the boat is back up to speed.

Fully hiked for a flat spot

Steer into the tack

As the boat comes flat pass back foot over the toe strap

Duck under boom

Keep mainsheet tight with right hand

Ease the sheet slightly as you cross the boat

Jump out on the new tack to pull the boat flat

Once the boat is flat sheet in slightly

Steer straight with the hand behind the back

Pull the mainsheet across your body towards the tiller

Grab the tiller with the mainsheet hand and hold both tiller and sheet in right hand

Pass your left arm around the body and grab the mainsheet. Sail away.

5 Basic Manoeuvres

The Gybe

For some, gybing is more feared than tacking and this may be because of the speed at which the boom crosses the boat. It is a faster movement and so timing is more critical. Unlike tacking there is always pressure in the sail so steering and body movements need to be more accurate especially in stronger winds. If the boat is going fast the pressure in the sail will be reduced making the manoeuvre easier.

Quick guide

Check to leeward and under the boom that it is clear to gybe.

Before entering the gybe check that there is not going to be any sudden change in wind or wave conditions.

As you bear away ease the sheet and keep the boat flat.

Sheet in slightly as you steer the boat into the gybe.

Steer smoothly into the gybe, as the sail starts to gybe straighten the tiller.

Start to move smoothly under the boom before it passes the centreline.

Sit on the new side and change hands bringing the mainsheet hand to the tiller hand.

Trim the mainsheet.

Check to leeward that it is clear to gybe

Bring the boat flat and sheet in slightly

Start to bear away rolling the boat to windward

Allow the boat to roll more

As the boom starts to roll reach across with the tiller hand

Before the boom crosses the centreline the body should have crossed the boat

Start to pull the boat flat to prevent the boom from hitting the water

Pull the boat flat

Start to straighten up the tiller and level the boat

Bring the mainsheet hand to the tiller and change hands

Swing the tiller around in front of the body and trim the sail

5   Basic Manoeuvres

Gybing in strong winds

Gybing can become difficult when the wind is blowing harder, so the first thing to do is to stop the boat taking over, ask yourself: "Are you riding or are you driving?" When it gets so windy that gybes become difficult the following techniques need to be used.

Quick guide

As you approach the gybe bear away beyond a broad reach.

Make sure you are in control of the boat and the boat is settled.

When the boat is at full speed pick a wave and a spot to gybe, if the boat is slow there will be more power in the rig making things more difficult.

Sheet in slightly and if unsure when the boom will cross, watch the leech of the sail between the top two battens as you bear away, as when the leech reacts to the turning it starts to fold. When you start to bear away the boat will roll to windward slightly, pull the mainsheet hard to initiate the gybe and as soon as the sail starts to move across the boat hold the tiller straight to reduce the angle of the turn. Quickly start to change sides and straighten the tiller.

If you can anticipate this start to move sides earlier.

Try to exit the gybe closer to a run than a reach. This helps the stability as all the power in the sail is pushing the boat forward along its axis and not over to the side. If the boat becomes side on to the wind the chance of capsize is high.

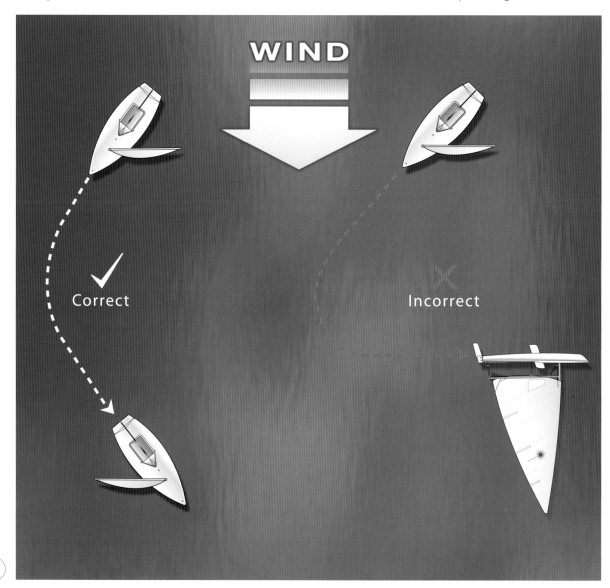

Settle the boat and make sure you're in control

Heel the boat to windward slightly and sheet in

Initiate the turn with the tiller, as the boat passes through downwind start to cross

Quickly cross the boat and commit to new side

Steer the boat straight with your hand behind your back

Bring the mainsheet hard to the tiller and hold both, maintaining a straight course

Swing the tiller around the body and trim the sail

5 Basic Manoeuvres

Light winds run to run gybing

Gybing in lighter winds without steering and while going straight can be a tactical advantage to keep clear air behind.

Quick guide

To gybe the boat in lighter winds without steering you need to physically pull the mainsheet across the boat with your hand, using the end of the tiller extension to collect the mainsheet.

Grab this with your front hand.

Bear away slightly and roll the boat as you pull the rope over your head.

Release the mainsheet after the boom passes over your head and you change sides. Try and keep the sheet high to avoid it catching the water. Release when there is wind filling the sail and the boat is heeled to windward.

Change hands and settle on the new gybe.

1 Sail slightly up the lee

2 Swing the tiller extension under the mainsheet

3 Lift the extension to collect the rope

4 Reach inboard and grab the mainsheet

5 Bear away slightly and roll the boat windward

6 As the boat rolls pull hard on the mainsheet to bring the sail across the boat

7 *Duck under the boom*

8 *Straighten the tiller as the boom passes overhead*

9 *Hold the mainsheet to stop it catching the water*

10 *As the boom reaches the new side start to cross the boat*

11 *Steer straight with your hand behind your back*

12 *Release the sheet as you sit on the new side*

13 *Change hands and take the mainsheet from the ratchet block*

14 *Heel the boat to windward and swing the extension round in front of the body*

Common Problems

Getting the mainsheet caught on the transom

The most common problem with gybing in the Laser is the mainsheet getting caught around the transom corners. This usually occurs when the action is not smooth, and a smooth course has not been steered, so remember to steer a smooth course and any change in heel should be gradual to prevent the mainsheet becoming caught.

Occasionally the mainsheet will get caught around the transom, it is important to clear this as quickly as possible without slowing the boat down.

1. If the mainsheet gets caught then it can be removed from the corner by simply grabbing the mainsheet, another technique to consider is using the tiller extension to free the sheet by swinging it around the transom. To clear the mainsheet swing the tiller around the transom, looping the mainsheet on the tiller extension.

2. Pull hard to remove the sheet from under the gunwale.

3. As the sheet is released swing the tiller back around to in front of the body and sail away. See picture (3)

The kicker is as important for gybing as for tacking. If the kicker is too loose the leech of the sail will be even further out than the boom, (known as twist). For the boat to gybe a much larger angle will have to be sailed to get the wind to catch the new side of the sail. Gybing with too much kicker tension can be dangerous as it will be difficult to avoid the boom and the chance of it catching in the water on the new gybe is much higher.

Getting caught in Irons

Irons is when the boat becomes stuck between tacks and is unable to sail forward. In stronger winds it is easy to get caught in irons and loose steerage. The quickest and easiest way to get out of this is to simply ease the mainsheet and push the tiller away from you. The boat will travel backwards and bear away until the sail fills again. Try to resist wiggling the tiller to bear away as this is not as efficient. If the boat is getting caught in irons regularly, try to ease the kicker slightly.

6   Racing Manoeuvres

See Training Exercises 1 & 5

Windward mark rounding

The fleet is usually very tight at the windward mark so it is good to plan your approach in advance. If you are not in the leading group of boats it is best to avoid getting to the lay line too early as it is inevitable that one of the leaders will tack on or in front of you, giving you dirty air or causing you to tack out and over stand the mark, sailing more distance.

Before arriving at the windward mark you need to decide which way you want to go on the next leg, as this will affect how critical the rounding will be. If the next leg of the course is a tight reach, or you want to go right looking down the run, then you need to make sure that you are on the outside at the mark to get the best set up for the next leg. If you want to go low on the next reach or left on the run looking downwind, then it is important to round as close to the buoy as possible. All of this changes our approach.

Quick guide

Approaching on starboard

As you approach the mark the loose end of the mainsheet needs to be freed from around your feet to ensure that there are no tangles and the mainsheet can be eased when needed.

In light winds ease the Cunningham at three boat lengths, in stronger winds leave the Cunningham on until after the rounding as this will help keep the leech open and assist the bear away.

At two boat lengths away the kicker should be released.

Ease the blocks slightly from block to block to allow the kicker to release.

Heel the boat to windward and start to release the sheet as the bow passes the buoy (heeling the boat to windward slightly will help reduce the loads on the tiller and assist the boat turning).

Continue to ease the sheet.

On a downwind course release the outhaul, re-trim the kicker and lift the daggerboard, if necessary adjust the toe strap.

Approaching on port

If approaching the mark on port within two boat lengths of the mark and have time the kicker should be released before the tack, this will make the bear away easier.

1 Free up as much of the loose mainsheet as possible

2 Keeping the boat flat reach in to release the Cunningham

3 Ease the mainsheet slightly & release the kicker (The mainsheet needs to be released to allow the boom to rise)

4 Ease the mainsheet and heel the boat to windward to assist the turn

5 *Sit back to lift the bow and help the mainsheet release, keep the boat heeled to windward*

6 *Move back forward as you reach a downwind course*

7 *Release the outhaul*

8 *Lift the daggerboard*

9 *Re-trim the kicker*

10 *Make sure the Cunningham is completely released*

6 Racing Manoeuvres

See Training Exercises 2 & 5

Leeward mark rounding

If a gate is used at the leeward mark it is important to decide early on the run which side of the gate you want to round because this will affect the final approach. If the gate is heavily biased it is more crucial to get the right one. The bias of the gate is similar to the bias of a start line, the buoy that is further to windward is the favoured end. If you have a definite race plan for the beat, for example you want to go right, then it may be worth giving away a bit of bias to take the correct gate which will get you to that side of the course.

The approach to a single leeward mark is more critical, if you get the approach wrong to a gate you can always bail out and go round the other buoy. A good rounding is important to give you a tactically commanding position, and will give you clear air and a good set up for the next leg of the course. If the mark is busy and crowded it is worth slowing the boat down and waiting your turn so you can round next to the mark. It very rarely pays to sail around the outside of a bunch.

To make the best exit from the mark you will need to use a wide entrance to get a tight exit.

A poor rounding can reduce the tactical options for the next leg, which can then lead to big losses. To make the rounding easier approach on the same tack as the one you will exit the mark on. In an ideal world you would be on the right gybe to round the mark. We will first look at a rounding entering on the same tack as you leave.

Quick guide

Approaching the mark on the gybe you wish to exit, look to come from a wide position.

Ten boat lengths away, adjust the toe strap.

Five boat lengths adjust the outhaul using the calibration on the boom to replicate the setting from the previous upwind leg.

Two boat lengths adjust the Cunningham (the controls are adjusted in this sequence as this has the least effect on speed).

One boat length pull on the kicker slightly (the kicker is needed to aid the boat's speed while rounding giving the sail some power when it is sheeted in).

Heel the boat to leeward to assist the turn and aim to pass close to the buoy sheeting hand over hand.

Pull the boat flat and sheet block to block.

Re-trim the kicker.

If you need to gybe at the buoy, make sure that the controls are on early, if windy leave the kicker until after the gybe. If possible gybe just before the buoy, this helps with a smooth turn. Once the gybe is complete change hands quickly and sheet in as fast as possible.

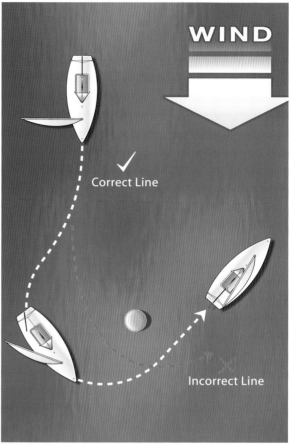

How to approach and exit the leeward mark

1 Get on the correct gybe early

2 Push the daggerboard down

3 *Pull the outhaul on using the boom calibration to replicate settings*

4 *Pull the Cunningham in early and leaning your body back to assist*

5 *Coming from wide snug up the kicker and start to sheet in*

6 *Heel the boat to leeward to assist the turn*

7 *Sheet in quickly as you turn around the buoy*

8 *Sheet block to block as you pull the boat flat*

9 *Pull on the kicker to the desired tension*

6 Racing Manoeuvres

See Training Exercise 1

Starting Manoeuvres

Acceleration

The ability to accelerate well is crucial for getting off the start line. It is good to practise holding position and then accelerating because this will replicate what happens in most starts. The key to acceleration is timing. The boat needs to be steered below a close-hauled course to help the boat accelerate forward. If you try to accelerate on a close-hauled course the boat will slide sideways until the flow can attach around the foils and give the boat some grip. Pulling the bow below a close-hauled course increases the acceleration by attaching flow to the foils quickly creating more lift and therefore grip for sailing to windward.

The first thing to do before accelerating is to pull the kicker on to the required tension for upwind sailing, this will help the boat accelerate.

To accelerate:

Quick guide

Pull the bow down away from the wind.

To bear away, jab the tiller to windward to start the bow coming down, keep the mainsheet eased.

As the bow comes below a close-hauled course heel the boat to leeward.

Bring the bow down to just below a close-hauled course.

Start to pull the boat flat while sheeting in (be careful not to pull the boat to windward).

Hold the bow just below a close-hauled course to build pace and flow over the foils.

As the speed increases bring the boat on to a close-hauled course and pull the last metre of the mainsheet in.

1 Reach forward and grab the kicker

2 Pull on the kicker to the upwind setting

3 Jab the tiller towards you to start the bear away

4 Heel the boat to windward and ease the mainsheet

5 As the boat passes below a close-hauled course flatten the boat

6 *Heel the boat to leeward and start to sheet in slowly*

7 *Sheet in a little more*

8 *Hike hard to flatten the boat and drive the boat forward*

9 *Once the boat is up to speed sheet block to block and return to a close hauled course*

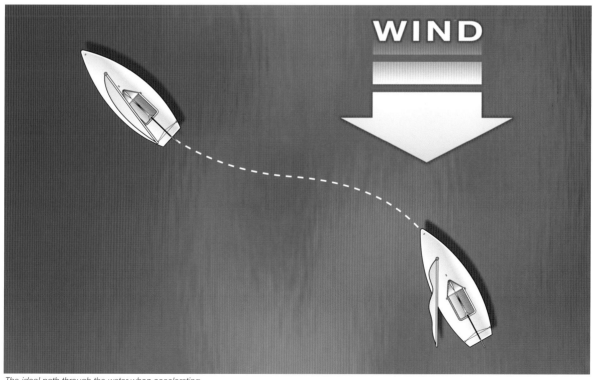

The ideal path through the water when accelerating

See Training Exercise 1

Holding position – hovering

It is inevitable that you will drift sideways while hovering and trying to hold position, minimising this drift will create a larger gap for you to accelerate into. When holding position practise close to a buoy so you can monitor your progress. It is important to make sure that the kicker is loose, if there is too much kicker tension the leech will be tight having the effect of sheeting the sail in, this will push the boat forward. If the kicker is loose the leech will just flap. While hovering it is important to keep the boat level as too much windward or leeward heel will increase the chance of sliding sideways. The boat should be kept on and just above a close-hauled course, sailing with the kicker off. This helps to stop the boat from going forward. The daggerboard should be kept fully down.

Checking the foils for weed

Strands of weed on the daggerboard

The 720 (Penalty Turn)

It is inevitable when racing that at some point we will need to take a penalty. It is worth taking a bit of time to practise linking up the tack and gybe because combined the entry is slightly different to the separate elements. While taking a penalty on a windward leg of the course it is important to minimise the distance lost downwind, this means the gybe needs to be completed as quickly as possible and time can be taken over the tack. When taking a penalty on a downwind leg it is the opposite.

Removing Weed from the foils

If the rudder or daggerboard are fouled with debris from the water the boat speed and pointing ability will be reduced, it is therefore important to remove any debris quickly, without losing too much speed or distance. To check for weed heel the boat slightly and look under the boat at the foils (1). The easiest way to remove weed from the daggerboard when sailing to windward is to head up into the wind, lift the board quickly and place back down before bearing away to accelerate. By doing it this way minimal distance is lost to leeward because the boat is travelling into the wind as the foil is cleared.

To clear the rudder, heel the boat to leeward and vigorously waggle the tiller, the weed should work its way down the blade and off the end. Clearing the blades will momentarily cause a small loss of speed but leaving the weed on will decrease the efficiency of the foils and slow the boat down, resulting in a greater loss.

Lift the board when the boat is luffting

7 Sailing Theory

There are several key ideas I refer to when thinking about making the boat go fast. If you understand the principles of what makes a boat go fast, then you have a better chance of being able to make it go fast. This understanding will also help to work out why the boat is slow when things aren't quite going to plan. Without getting too scientific the following will hopefully give a brief outline of what is happening to the boat while out on the water.

Tell Tales

These are your best tool to make sure you are trimming the sail properly. If the sail is over-sheeted the windward tell tale will fly and the leeward one stall. If under-sheeted the sail will flap or the leeward one will fly and the windward one will never fly. When sailing upwind the leeward tell tale should fly horizontally all of the time. The windward one should fly very occasionally when searching for speed and power. When reaching both tell tales should occasionally fly horizontally, the focus should be primarily on the leeward tell tale.

Downwind angles

Modern day Laser techniques when sailing downwind involve lots of turning to catch waves. It is generally faster to sail by the lee: this is when the wind flows from the leech of the sail to the luff rather than from the luff to the leech which is what happens while sailing upwind or on a reach (Boat A). It is important to know which way the air is flowing over the sail so it can be trimmed correctly. The best indication of flow is simply by looking at the tell tales and the direction they are pointing. Sailing the boat flat to the wind (Boat c) is generally slow as the flow around the sail stalls.

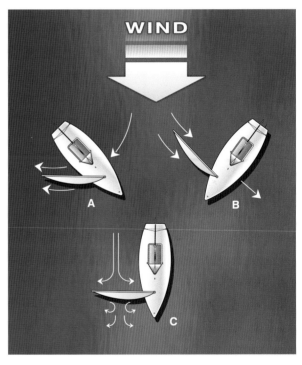

Boat A is sailing with correct flow. Boat B is sailing by the lee flow. Boat C has disturbed flow as the air cannot flow around the sail.

Tiller angle

You need to use the tiller most of the time to steer the boat, but the greater the tiller angle, the more drag is created by the rudder. To minimise the amount of rudder needed you can alter the trim and heel angle of the boat.

Heel angle

When the hull is flat in the water it is symmetrical, but when the boat heels it becomes non-symmetrical and wants to turn, the result of which is more drag.

The best way to understand this is by sailing without using the rudder. If the boat is heeled to windward the boat wants to bear away (2). If the boat is heeled to leeward the boat wants to luff in to the wind (1). We often don't realise that the rudder is being used all the time to keep the boat travelling in a straight line to compensate for the heel angle which causes extra drag and reduces the boat's speed.

The principles are the same when sailing upwind and downwind.

Fore and Aft trim

Body weight has the main effect on fore and aft trim. For each point of sailing and wind strength there will be an optimum angle of trim. In lighter winds it is important to sit forward to keep the transom out of the water. In stronger winds it is important to gain the maximum water line length and when planing we need to sit back to lift the bow clear of the water. If the boat is kept flat and stable the air flow over the sail and water flow around the rudder and daggerboard will remain constant. If the boat starts to move around more the flow over the foils and sail will be disturbed, creating a loss of lift and an increase in drag.

Proactive not Reactive

Before the boat is overpowered trim and heel are all down to body movements, once overpowered easing the sheet helps balance the boat. Quick body movements are often associated with good boat trim, while this helps it is more important to anticipate changes in wind and sea state; this will help you to make the adjustments before the conditions change and affect the boat.The helm needs to be proactive rather than reactive to help reduce sudden movements that will disturb the rig.

Focus

When racing, what you need to focus on changes depending on the situation. In tight situations such as off a start line you need to keep the focus narrow, concentrating on the boats next to you and keeping the boat going as fast as possible. In situations where the fleet is spread out and there are no boats close by, focus will need to be wide, concentrating on the position of the next mark, the fleet position and their relative angles. With experience it becomes easier to prioritise what you need to focus on and to quickly change focus.

Daggerboard position

The daggerboard is used to create lift helping the boat sail to windward and it should be all the way down while sailing upwind in all conditions. When sailing downwind the daggerboard is needed to help the boat track but has the adverse effect of creating drag. You therefore need to decide how much daggerboard to leave in the water without affecting the boat's track but at the same time minimising drag, while sailing downwind.

Advanced Sailing Theory

Lift and drag

I like to think about lift and drag when considering sail set. When the outhaul, kicker and Cunningham are loose this gives the sail more depth (also called camber). This sail shape will create more lift (see illustration boat 1). If the sail is flatter (less camber) (see illustration boat 2) then there is less lift produced. So why don't we always sail with a deep sail? When the sail has more camber it produces a lot of power and sometimes more than is needed. If the wind increases we require less power from the sail, too much power will just push the boat over sideways when sailing to windward. The downside of a fuller sail is that it creates more drag and it is harder for the air flow to stay attached around the sail especially in lighter winds. It is therefore important to get the right balance between lift and drag when setting the sail for the appropriate wind strength. I like to use my hand on the boom to check the depth of the outhaul. This can be done by placing your wrist at the boom cleat and seeing when your fingers touch the sail. Picture 1 shows a deep outhaul setting of just over a hand, picture 2 shows a flat sail. Remember that the rudder and daggerboard will also create lift. The faster the boat is travelling through the water the more lift the foils are creating, this is important to understand when sailing to windward. If you are going slower than normal speed for the given wind strength then the foils are less efficient, producing less lift, this will prevent the boat from sailing close to the wind because it will slip sideways.

Full sail, one hand depth, watch strap to fingers

Flat sail, palm to fingers

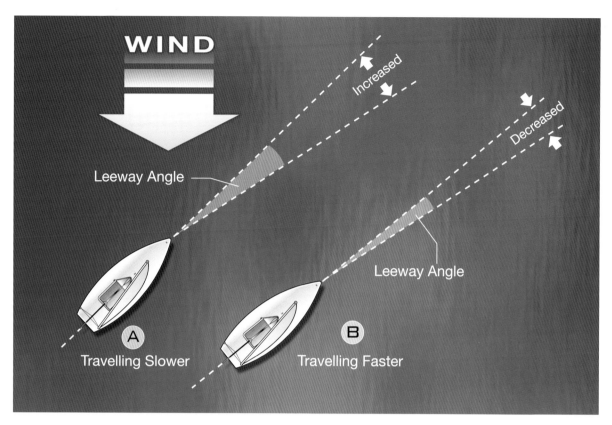

Leeway Angle

The direction that a boat is pointing might not necessarily be the course it is sailing due to its leeway angle. Lasers are not the most efficient boats when sailing to windward as they slip slightly sideways, the difference between the direction that the boat is pointing and the direction that the boat is travelling is the leeward angle. I like to refer to this as "grip", the better the foils are working the better grip we have and the leeway angle is reduced. When the boat speed is slow for a given wind strength or in choppy seas the boat will not track along the angle it is pointing, it will actually travel slightly sideways (B). At higher speeds for the given wind strength or in flat water the foils will be more efficient therefore creating more lift allowing the boat to travel closer to the angle it is pointing (A). It is important to be aware of this while sailing especially when trying to sail high or hold above another boat when sailing to windward. This is particularly evident out of a start when the boats are close. Often boats try to point too high before they are up to speed and end up sliding sideways towards the boat they are trying to hold away from.

8 Wind Categories

Beaufort Scale	Knots	Mph	Description	Effects at sea	Effects on land
0	0	0	Calm	Sea like a mirror	Smoke rises vertically
1	1-3	1-3	Light air	Ripples, but no foam crests	Smoke drifts in the wind
2	4-6	4-7	Light breeze	Small wavelets	Leaves rustle. Wind felt on face
3	7-10	8-12	Gentle breeze	Large wavelets crests not breaking	Small twigs in constant motion. Light flags extended
4	11-16	13-18	Moderate wind	Numerous whitecaps	Dust, leaves and loose paper raised. Small branches move
5	17-21	19-24	Fresh wind	Many whitecaps, some spray	Small trees sway
6	22-27	25-31	Strong wind	Larger waves form. Whitecaps everywhere. More spray	Large branches move. Whistling in phone wires. Difficult to use umbrellas
7	28-33	32-38	Very strong wind	White foam from breaking waves begins to be blown in streaks	Whole trees in motion
8	34-40	39-46	Gale	Edges of wave crests begin to break into spindrift	Twigs break off trees. Difficult to walk

Wind Categories

To make this easier to understand I have split the techniques and setup into three categories.

1 Light winds

2 Medium winds

3 Strong winds

These three categories will differ slightly depending on the size of the sailor.

• Light winds - 0 - 8 knots or until you are starting to hike properly not just perching on the side.

• Medium winds - 8 -16 knots or from when you start hiking to when you are overpowered and fully planing.

• Strong winds - 16+ knots or overpowered and fully planing.

When using the categories above try and use the wording rather than the wind speeds; the wind speeds should be about right for someone who is the optimum weight for the boat, if you are lighter than the optimum weight you will move up to the medium winds category at a lower wind speed, heavier and you will move up later.

9 Upwind Technique Set Up

"Good upwind pace can make you a tactical genius"

Having good speed to windward will make racing much easier, you will be able to escape from tight situations and get away with missing a shift and still be at the front of the fleet at the windward mark.

See Training Exercise 3

Light wind technique and set up

Sail settings

The sail needs to be set so that the wind can flow easily around it without losing any flow. To do this the mast needs to bend reducing the fullness at the front of the sail. If this is done by using the mainsheet alone the leech becomes very tight and hooked. By using the kicker the boom is forced into the mast causing the mast to bend even more and making the leech less hooked (see illustration page 36 kicker tension). There should be very little tension in the mainsheet while sailing because the boom will be held down by the kicker. There should be enough kicker to hold the blocks 20cm apart at the traveller. As the wind increases use more mainsheet tension to bring the blocks closer together. You should wait to go block to block until you are just starting to sit over the gunwale to maintain the boat's trim. The outhaul should be about 20cm deep at the outhaul boom cleat (just over one hand) see picture page 70, if the sail is too deep it will be difficult for the flow to stay attached, too flat and the lift will be reduced. Minimal Cunningham should be used (if any is needed), just use enough to pull the large diagonal creases out of the sail.

Technique

The key to light wind sailing is to keep the boat moving. Once the boat is moving well through the water you can start to head up slightly to gain height, before the boat slows bear away again to keep the boat up to speed. Be very careful not to go too high for too long, once the boat has stalled it is very difficult to get the boat back up to speed. The boat should be steered up and down very subtly gaining height to windward when possible and then driving for speed when you feel the boat is beginning to slow.

Try to be as subtle as possible with all body movements and steering, in flat water once the boat is up to speed try and let the boat sail itself with minimal input. In choppy conditions try and steer around any bad waves and concentrate on keeping the boat moving at all times. If the boat stalls bear away slightly and allow the pressure in the rig to build then pull the boat flat by leaning the upper body back, this will accelerate the boat.

Keep any movements to a minimum and any needed should be smooth and gentle. Sharp movements will disturb the flow of wind over the sail and the water flow over the daggerboard, both essential for efficient upwind sailing.

Keep the trim constant with a slight heel to leeward (less than 10 degrees), this will help to give the rudder some feel. Maintain body weight far enough forward in the boat to keep the transom just clear of the water which will help reduce the wetted surface area of the boat and therefore drag.

In flat water it can help to have the boat dead flat, this will give the rig more power, if there is any change in pressure the boat is in danger of coming to windward, this will induce lee helm which is slow. In choppier conditions leeward heel is preferred making it easier to steer and reducing the risk of windward heel.

The biggest mistake is sailing with the front of the sail curling, it is important to use all the power that is available in light winds. Other common mistakes are sailing with the boat heeled to windward and the mainsheet too tight.

Using the tiller behind you gives you more accuracy

An ideal upwind sail set and heel angle

Medium wind technique and set up

In these conditions there can be large differences in water conditions, anything from flat water to large swells. In flatter water the speed differences are very small but in waves where technique plays a part the differences can be much bigger. In flat water the boat requires very little steering and body movement and can basically sail itself.

Sail Settings

To get maximum power out of the rig in medium winds, you will need to have maximum leech tension, this is achieved by using mainsheet tension only. If the kicker is used the leech tension will be reduced as the boom will be pushed into the mast causing it to bend and therefore losing leech tension. As the boat starts to get overpowered increase the kicker tension to bend the mast, flatten the sail and release the leech tension. The outhaul should be set at about 10–15cm deep (about a hand's width) at the boom cleat and the Cunningham should be pulled tight enough to remove most of the diagonal creases from the sail. As you start to become overpowered the Cunningham and kicker should be used progressively to depower the rig. Once the Cunningham has removed all the creases then the outhaul should start to be tightened.

In marginal hiking conditions the mainsheet can pull the boom towards the centreline of the traveller. It is really important to have the traveller as tight as possible to help stop this. If the boom still slides inboard use your foot to push the boom back to the edge; when the boom is inboard the sheeting angle is changed causing the leech to hook more. As the wind strength increases, the centre of effort quickly moves back in the sail (especially in older sails), use the Cunningham to pull it forward. If the boat is experiencing a lot of weather helm you probably need more Cunningham or to sail the boat flatter.

Technique

The boat should be sailed upright in flat water and you should ideally be sitting with your front leg next to the mainsheet cleat (1). As the waves increase sail with slightly more heel (2). If there are more than a couple of waves in each beat washing over the deck, move back slightly in the cockpit, if no waves are coming over the bow sit slightly forward. Try and maintain a constant speed through the water. In the flatter water sail slightly higher than in choppier sections. Try and avoid choppy sections of water by looking ahead and altering course to try and avoid any bad waves. If you have to sail through some bad waves bear away to accelerate the boat to push through the waves.

When sailing upwind with a new sail, and starting to use the kicker, the bottom batten can invert, so keep checking the sail especially when working the boat very hard. If the sail starts to invert, ease the kicker and stop working the boat as hard – remember if the sail is inverting the boat is losing power and will sail lower and slower.

Try and maintain the boat's trim by moving fore and aft

A good sail set and keel angle

Body movements in waves

In waves the boat needs a lot more input. It is important to have the toe strap set to the right length so that any body movements can be transferred through the boat (see Hiking chapter).

The steering and body movements need to be linked together, this way less rudder is needed to steer the boat. Look at the waves ahead, as a wave approaches lean back and head up slightly (2), this will lift the bow and accelerate the boat forward, as the bow comes over the top of the wave lean the body back upright or even slightly forward (1) and bear away to power down the back of the wave.

The speed of these movements is determined by the waves, in large swells these movements are slower and smoother to synchronise with the waves, in choppier conditions these movements need to be quicker and sharper to force the boat through the chop.

Leaning forward to bear away

Leaning back to head up and lift the bow

Strong wind technique and set up

Technique

This can be the most physically challenging part of Laser sailing, as soon as you ease back the boat will slow and slip sideways. It is just as important in strong winds to keep the boat speed up as it is in light winds. The most common problem especially in waves is to try and sail the boat too high and pinch, the boat will sail slow, stall and slip sideways. (See leeway angle illustration page 71). Try and keep the boat driving as much as possible, this will require you to hike hard and ease a lot of sheet to keep the boat flat.

Trim is really important in strong winds because it is difficult to keep the boat flat. Look to windward and try to anticipate the gusts so you can be proactive rather than reactive. If a gust is coming towards you, be ready to ease the mainsheet and hike harder, in flatter water you can also head up slightly using the tiller to help keep the boat flat. Once the boat heels over the foils are less efficient and the boat starts to slip sideways reducing the vmg.

When it's really windy the mainsheet can be eased as much as one metre between the traveller blocks, remember it is more important to keep the boat moving fast through the water than trying for height especially in rough seas. It is easy to fill the cockpit with water in these conditions, to help the cockpit drain more efficiently remove the bung from the bailer and store under the grab rail.

A good upwind sail set, note the mainsheet is eased to help keep the boat flat and driving

9 Upwind Technique Set Up

Sail settings

In strong winds you will need to de-power the rig as much as possible. The Cunningham should be pulled hard on a new sail until the cringle touches the gooseneck (3). On an older sail the Cunningham needs to be rigged to one side of the boom (1), this allows it to be pulled below the top of the gooseneck and more tension to be gained (see photo). A problem with doing this is the sail will have a different depth on each tack so the outhaul may need to be adjusted tack to tack.

The kicker needs to be tight to flatten the sail and to stop the blocks from rising when the mainsheet is eased. Photo 3 shows a good kicker tension as the blocks travel horizontally when eased. This keeps the sail flat and a similar shape. Photo 4 shows the blocks rising vertically, this causes the sail to change shape increasing the depth in the top of the sail causing the boat to heel over more. Have the kicker as tight as possible up to the point where it becomes difficult to cross the boat during tacks. The outhaul should be used to flatten the bottom of the sail, try to resist pulling it bar tight as the sail still needs a bit of shape low down; about 5-10 cm between the boom cleat and sail is enough.

Cunningham rigged one side max on

Cunningham rigged both sides max on

Bung removed to help the cockpit drain

Good kicker tension/boom low

Not enough kicker, boom too high

Full Rig Sail Settings Matrix

| | Upwind | | | |
	Light	Medium	Strong	Light
Kicker	Less than block to block allowing the boom to rise so there is up to 30 cm between the blocks	Block to block	More than block to block to stop the blocks from rising when the mainsheet is eased	Loose to allow the leech to fan up to 30 cm either side of neutral
Cunningham	Eased	Just enough to remove the major diagonal creases, increase tension as the wind increases	On hard down to gooseneck or one side on older sails	Eased
Outhaul	20 cm deep at boom cleat, just over one hand	15 cm deep at boom cleat or a hand width	5-10 cm deep at boom cleat	Eased up to 25 cm
Mainsheet	Between 10 - 30 cm between the blocks ensuring the blocks are wide on the traveller	Block to block	Play the mainsheet in the gusts between block to block and 1 m between the blocks ensuring there is enough kicker tension to stop the blocks from rising when the main is eased	Allow the boom out as far as 90-110 degrees
Daggerboard	Down	Down	Down	Up 15 - 20 cm
Body Position	Forward by the daggerboard	Just behind the side deck cleat	Up to 15 cm behind the side deck cleat	Forward by the daggerboard
Trim	5-10 degrees leeward heel	Up to 5 degrees leeward heel	Flat	10-20 degrees windward heel
Tips	Keep all movements smooth	Hike hard to drive the boat	Anticipate the gusts and ease the sheet to maintain a constant heel angle	Keep all movements smooth

	Downwind		Reaching		
	Medium	**Strong**	**Light**	**Medium**	**Strong**
	oose enough to allow 30 cm of twist at the top of the sail	Loose enough to allow up to 30 degrees of twist	Just enough to bend the mast slightly flattening the entry	Set the leech slightly twisted matching the top and bottom tell tales. Boom just less than 90 degrees to mast	Loose to stop the boom tripping in the water and allow excess power to be released
	Eased	Eased	Eased	Eased	Eased, but may be needed when overpowered on tight reaches
	sed up to 20 cm	Eased up to 15 cm	15 cm deep	20 cm deep	10 -15 cm deep
	ow the boom no further than 90 degrees	Allow the boom out to 75 - 85 degress	Trim to the leeward tell tales	Trim to both tell tales	Trim to the leeward tell tales
	Jp 15 - 20 cm	Up 15 - 20 cm	Up 15 - 20 cm	Up 20 - 25 cm	Up 20 - 25 cm
	Move back as the boat starts to celerate and plane nd then when the t slows move your ght forward again.	Sit as far back as possible to lift the bow	Forward by the daggerboard	Move back as the boat starts to accelerate and plane and then when the boat slows move your weight forward again.	Sit as far back as possible to lift the bow
	to 10 degrees vindward heel	Flat	5-10 degrees leeward heel	Up to 5 degrees leeward heel	Flat
	quick to move vard as the boat ows and head up slightly	Keep either by the lee or on a broad reach, don't let the mainsheet out too far	Keep all movements smooth	Keep a constant heel angle by playing the mainsheet	Anticipate and bear away in the gusts

10 Hiking

Hiking is essential for good upwind speed in a Laser and there are many different styles and techniques that all work, but it is down to you to use what is the most comfortable and effective.

Different conditions require different styles of hiking. In flat water you are just trying to achieve the maximum righting moment which will give the boat greater drive. This is achieved by trying to get the shoulders as far as possible away from the gunwale and creating a large righting moment (2). When the water becomes choppy and the waves start to increase you need to be able to move your body both fore and aft to maintain the fore and aft trim of the boat as it sails through the water. I feel that when I am creating the largest righting moment in flat water my body is restricted in the fore and aft plane. In waves I therefore adopt a hiking position where my body is less extended and slightly upright, this increases my mobility and allows me to move my body fore and aft (3).

To gain a good posture and achieve a good hiking shape you need to keep your legs straight and lean the shoulders back, being careful not to hyper-extend.

The illustrations show three different body positions:

Fig 1 shows a common mistake: you may feel that you are hiking really hard but, because your bottom is a long way from the gunwale but the body position from the hips to the shoulders is nearly vertical, you are not generating a good lever.

Fig 2 shows straighter legs with the bottom further inboard and with the shoulders leaning back towards horizontal. This creates a better lever and a more effective hiking position. This position is suitable for flatter water.

Fig 3 shows the toe strap a little longer and the legs are bent slightly helping to create a bit more mobility for the upper body. The shoulders are not as flat as fig 2 and can therefore easily be moved forward and to help steer the boat through waves.

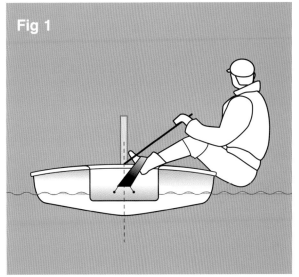

Fig 1

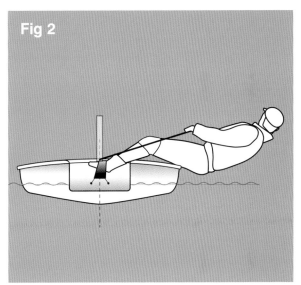

Fig 2

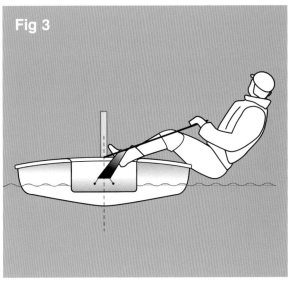

Fig 3

10 Hiking

Toe strap length

The length a strap should be depends on how tall you are and in an ideal world the toe strap would be tight to help keep the legs straight and the bottom out of the water. If you are under 1.82mtrs (6 feet) tall you will need to lengthen the toe strap to allow the body to get further out of the boat and adjust your posture a little as it will be harder to stay straight legged. To check your toe strap length push or pull the toe strap towards the grabrail (1). Do not go longer than the toe strap touching the grabrail.

Check the length of toe strap by pulling against the grab rail

A good hiking posture - note the knee and hip angles

Hiking moves

There are several set moves that are used when hiking to get the most upwind performance from the boat. A basic understanding of what you are trying to achieve is necessary to know what is the right move at the right time when out on the water.

Bouncing

This is a body movement to windward and away from the boat. What happens when the body is thrown to windward is that a greater force is created on the side of the boat pushing the windward side down. The bounce also affects the sail shape as the movement causes the mast to bend sideways; this then causes the upper leech of the sail to fall away releasing power from the sail. I use this movement when I am overpowered and need to release pressure from the sail and it helps to drive the boat forward. Caution: when racing repeated movements in this motion are illegal so it is only used when overpowered.

Moving the shoulders aft

Used mainly when sailing in waves it can help to lift the bow over a bad wave but can also be used to stop the bow from slamming into the water when the bow goes over a wave. It also has the effect of lifting the bow and pulling it to windward so effectively steering the boat, pushing the tiller away has a similar effect. I use this technique to stop the boat from slamming into waves and reduce the pitching effect of chop.

Moving the shoulders forward

Helps to keep the bow in the water and stops the wind from blowing it around and also has the effect of bearing the boat away and sticking the bow into the water - pulling the tiller towards you has a similar effect. I use this move more in steep chop when the bow can spend a lot of time in the air when going over the tops of waves.

To make the body movements fore and aft effective, the feet should stay in the same position under the toe strap during the whole movement. The longer the toe strap the harder it is to torque the boat using your upper body because the feet tend to move around in the cockpit and the upper body movements cannot be transmitted through the boat. If this is the case the toe strap needs to be tightened. See Body movements in waves (page 78) for more details of linking these moves together.

11 Downwind Sailing

Having good boat speed downwind is essential if you are going to win races, it is also a great way of escaping from the middle of the fleet back to the leading bunch. Sailing the shortest route to the mark is very rarely the fastest, by sailing larger angles downwind you can achieve greater speeds and have the ability to catch waves. The most important sail control downwind is the kicker, by sailing with a looser kicker the boat becomes more versatile helping it to accelerate out of changes in course.

To help catch waves you nearly have to forget about the direction of the next mark, just concentrate on catching waves and surfing them for as long as possible.

See Training Exercise 4

Running in light winds

Sail Settings
The kicker should be loose enough to enable the top of the sail to twist away and to flex. This helps the sail react to gusts and alterations in course without you needing to adjust the mainsheet. As the leech moves the sail pants and the boat is propelled forward, the outhaul should now be as loose as it ever needs to be with just over a hand's width between the foot of the sail and the boom cleat; this creates power and drive in the lower third of the sail. Ease the Cunningham to allow fullness in the sail. The critical control is the kicker and this should be set "by eye". When sailing by the lee, look at the leech around the top batten, this area of the sail should be able to move between 10 and 30 cm fore and aft. If the leech is tight and the movement is restricted ease the kicker and if it is moving more than 30 cm, tighten the kicker slightly.

Technique
In light winds it is important to keep all movements slow and smooth to keep the wind in the sail stable and attached, if the boat is rocking around then the air flow over the sail will be disrupted and this will cause the sail to lose drive. Sailing by the lee is often faster in light winds, the boat needs to be heeled slightly to windward, to reduce the wetted surface area, this also helps gravity to keep the boom out. Your body weight should be kept forward in the cockpit to keep the transom clear of the water and the daggerboard should be raised around 15 cm, this helps the boat to track in a straight line when sailing large angles by the lee.

Boat speed in these conditions will be determined by wind speed more than technique, be observant and keep looking behind for wind. When sailing in a gust the boat can be sailed closer to a downwind course, as the wind drops steer back towards a bigger angle by the lee.

Correct kicker tension allowing sail to twist

Boat heeled to windward slightly

11 Downwind Sailing

Running in medium winds

Sail Settings

The sail settings are very similar to light wind settings, again the kicker being the most crucial. The mainsheet no longer needs to be eased beyond 90 degrees as there will be more pressure in the sail causing the top to twist open, the top of the sail can twist beyond 100 degrees of the centreline even when the boom is at 80 degrees.

Technique

As the wind increases and the boat starts to plane the weight needs to move back in the boat, this helps to keep the bow clear of the waves. In marginal planing conditions the weight should be moved forward as the boat slows and aft as the boat accelerates.

When sailing in waves steer the boat onto different angles to help catch waves and increase speed. When the boat changes direction trim the mainsheet to compensate for the change in direction. To change direction try to use the heel of the boat to assist the turn, heeling the boat to leeward to head up, and leaving the boat to windward to help bear away. This will reduce the amount of rudder needed.

Note the boom is not at 90° but the top of the sail is due to the twist

Goodies Guide for sailing on a run

- As the boat slows the angle to the wind needs to decrease; do this by either bearing the boat away more to sail by the lee, or by sailing higher towards a reach.

- When the boat accelerates the speed needs to be turned into vmg and the boat should be sailed more downwind.

- The daggerboard should only be raised 15 cm so that the boat can track in a straight line.

11 Downwind Sailing

Running in strong winds

Sail Settings

In strong winds it is less important to ease the outhaul as you are not looking for any extra drive from the sail. It is however important to release the Cunningham and the kicker. If the Cunningham is left on then the leech will be really soft and will lead to too much twist in the head of the sail, this leaves the boat difficult to sail and often causes the boat to capsize to windward. If the kicker is not released then the boat is very twitchy because the leech is unable to soak up changes in steering and wind, leading the boat tripping and spinning into the wind and capsizing to leeward. Ease the kicker again so the leech moves up to 30 cm or 12 inches remembering that this is a much tighter kicker due to there being more pressure in the sail. The outhaul can be left in its upwind setting. By releasing the Cunningham the outhaul will automatically become slightly fuller.

Technique

Sheet the mainsheet in slightly to help stability, the boom angle should be around 70 degrees but the top of the sail about 95 degrees as the leech twists away.

Try not to run dead downwind, steer positively so that you are either by the lee or on a broad reach and sit back as far as you can. It can often help if you hold the tiller extension at the tiller to extension flexi-joint which will give a more positive feel to the rudder.

If things start to get a bit hairy then sit tight and try to keep the boat in a straight line, sheeting the mainsheet in by about a metre. The worse thing you can do is sheet out or alter course as this makes the boat unstable and uncontrollable because all the forces are moving. The daggerboard again should only be raised up to 20 cm to help tracking and in the worst case scenario there will be something to stand on if things go wrong!

The boom is at 70 degrees with a lot of leech twist

Nose dive

At some point it will be impossible to avoid running into the backs of waves or nose diving. The best thing to do is to hold tight as you run into the back of the wave (1) brace yourself and try and keep the boat heading in the same direction. As the water washes over the deck (2) it is important to hold the mainsheet tight as the pressure in the rig will greatly increase as the boat slows. Lean back and hopefully the bow will come clear and you can sail away (3). It is important to try and clear the cockpit of the excess water as quickly as possible to reduce the chance of it happening again, it will be more balanced and less likely to capsize.

Holding the tiller at the base gives more control over the rudder

11 Downwind Sailing

The kicker is the key control for the sail downwind, get it right and the boat can become easy to steer and stable, get it wrong and the boat becomes very twitchy and difficult to control.

1. Shows the kicker set too tight. The sail becomes flatter and the leech very tight. It becomes very difficult to be accurate with the sheeting angle as there is margin for error, any small steering alteration will change the entry and exit from the sail greatly.

2. Shows the kicker too loose. It is now very difficult to get the correct sheeting angle at the top and bottom of the sail because there is such a difference between the two. This usually leads to the boat becoming very rocky and power is lost from the top of the sail.

3. Shows an ideal kicker tension. The sail is full with enough twist to allow the leech to react to changes in course without losing any power out of the sail.

Running general principles

By the lee

When sailing by the lee the flow of air over the sail is changing; the flow is going from the leech to the luff (A). A common mistake often made when sailing by the lee is to let the boom out too far. If the sail is let out beyond 100 degrees then it will be hard to get the flow to change direction. If the boom is at 90 degrees then the top of the sail can be way beyond this when the kicker is eased. The best way to check the flow direction is by looking at the tell tales on the sail and seeing which way they are pointing. See illustration 4.

Sailing in gusty conditions

If you sail in a gust of stronger wind for longer downwind you are going to be quicker to the leeward mark. You need to check the wind regularly to see if there is any change in pressure that you can take advantage of (see picture 5). If a gust is coming from one side of the course sail to the gust and then in the gust for as long as possible. This will usually involve altering course to sail in the direction that the gust is travelling. Using a wind indicator gives a good indication of where the wind is coming from, by looking in the direction that the wind indicator is pointing you can anticipate the wind coming. Illustration 6 shows an ideal path in gusty conditions.

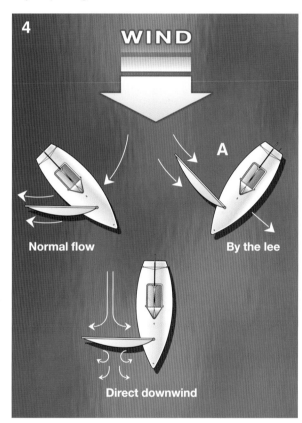

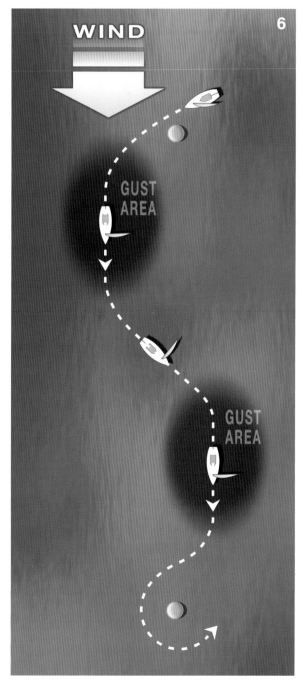

Keep checking the breeze behind

11 Downwind Sailing

Advanced wave principles

Waves are not all the same and this be can used to our advantage. I like to think of sailing downwind in waves as being similar to travelling on an escalator. Going down the run on the same wave it's as if you are standing stationary on the escalator. If you let the waves go underneath the boat then it is like stepping backwards on the escalator and if you get onto the wave in front it is like stepping forward. To be the fastest we need to try and make the most steps forward but this is not always possible and changes with the wind strength. In strong winds the objective is to make as many forward steps as possible and in light winds try to reduce the backward steps. So how do we do this?

Travelling down the wave on its steepest part will gain the most acceleration and by going up the wave on its flattest part there will be the least deceleration.

It is not possible to catch every wave so it is important to be patient and selective when choosing which one to go for. When you try and catch a wave and miss it you will go slower than a sailor that has just gone straight.

Catching the right waves you can ride for a longer period of time which is much better than riding four waves for a short period. To catch a wave you have selected you need to sail closer to the wind, either more by the lee or on a tighter reach. This will power the boat up and increase the speed, once the wave comes sail in the direction it is travelling and this may mean altering course. By using your weight to steer the boat less rudder is needed and the ride on the wave will be longer, so try and go with the wave whichever way it is taking you as this will help prolong the ride.

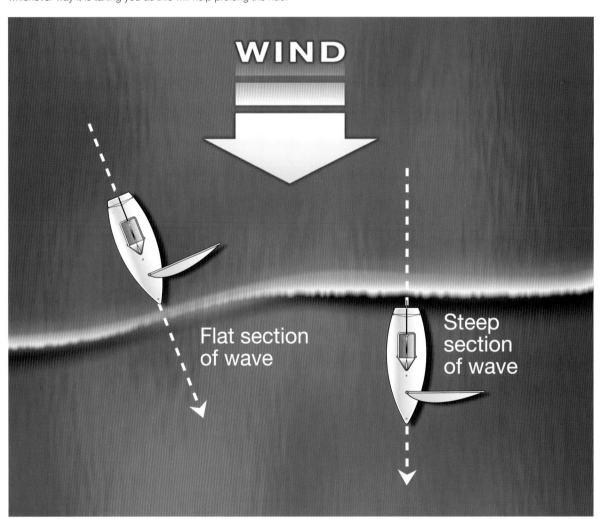

WIND

Flat section of wave

Steep section of wave

When the boat is trying to catch or surf on a wave it can be turned in one of two directions. I like to call these upturns when you head up towards a reach, and downturns when you bear away by the lee.

Upturns

To help the boat to turn it is important that the boat is heeled to leeward, so lift your weight from the windward side to help the boat heel. As the boat starts to heel head up slightly, as you start to head up sheet in to keep the sail pulling (see photo 2). Flatten the boat to squirt the boat forward down the wave (see photo 3), don't let the boat come beyond upright.

Downturns

Before you start to turn let the boat roll to windward (see photo 4), as the boat starts to roll bear away down the wave to the desired course; you may need to lean inboard to stop the boat rolling any further (see photo 5). As you accelerate down the wave lean inboard to flatten the boat slightly and re-trim the main (see photo 6), it will probably need to be eased slightly.

12 Sailing on a Reach

Reaching can be one of the most exhilarating parts of Laser sailing. It can also be one of the most frustrating as there are large speed differences between getting it right and wrong.

Basic reaching principles

When setting the rig I like to bear the following in mind: as the reach gets tighter the controls also need to become tighter mainly the kicker, outhaul and mainsheet. As the reach gets broader and away from the wind the controls become looser. In stronger winds it is slightly different but this is a good general principle.

Advanced reaching principles

When reaching the kicker and mainsheet are the most important sail controls because they have the biggest effect on speed. The kicker is the most difficult setting to get right. I like to think of the kicker as a mainsheet for the top third of the sail, Without kicker tension the mainsheet has effectively been released with the top third of the sail, if this is done to extreme the top of the sail will flap. On the other hand when there is too much kicker tension then the top third has been oversheeted. The best way to demonstrate this is by using a tell tale at the top of the sail and using it the same as you would use the tell tales lower down. The kicker will have the same effect on the top tell tales as the mainsheet does on the lower ones.

I try to think of the kicker as an accelerator and also a limiter. If the kicker is tight then the boat can accelerate easily but the top speed will be limited. However if the kicker is looser the boat will have a faster top speed but will not accelerate as well.

Kicker too loose - open leech

Kicker too tight - hooked leech

Correct kicker tension

The pictures above show clearly the effect the kicker has on the sail shape.

1. Shows a loose kicker, the top of the sail is very open losing a lot of power.

2. Shows a tight kicker, the sail becomes much flatter and the leech becoming hooked creating a drag and slowing the boat down.

3. The correct kicker tension, the top of the sail has good shape and the wind can exit the sail cleanly while the sail retains the power.

Reaching in light winds

Sail Settings

The sail needs to generate power to propel the boat but if the outhaul is too deep then the air becomes detached from the sail easily causing a loss of power and an increase in drag. In light wind conditions the outhaul may need to be slightly tighter than the upwind setting. The Cunningham should be completely released therefore creating a smooth entry at the front of the sail. The kicker is used mainly to bend the mast so that the sail is not too full and round just behind the mast. If the kicker is too loose and the mast is straight, the sail is too deep for the air to flow around. It is better to use more kicker to bend the mast and flatten the front of the sail even if this means the leech is hooked slightly creating more drag. Twist at the top of the sail is sacrificed for a flatter entry.

Technique

Weight should be kept well forward to prevent the transom from dragging; the boat also needs a slight leeward heel to help the sail fill. The daggerboard should be raised approximately 15 cm. All movements should be kept smooth so as not to disturb the wind over the sail. As soon as the boat increases in speed bear away slightly to stay low, as the boat slows head up again to increase the speed.

Ideal kicker tension and boat trim

Sitting well forward

12 Sailing on a Reach

Reaching in medium winds

Sail Settings
As the wind increases the outhaul can be eased to generate more power and as the boat starts to plane the outhaul can be tightened. The kicker can also be eased slightly to create more twist. You are now trying to match the tell tales at the foot of the sail with the ones at the top by using the mainsheet and kicker. The Cunningham should be completely off.

Technique
The boat needs to be flatter and the weight to be moved back slightly to gain maximum waterline length. As the boat begins to accelerate and plane the weight can be moved backwards but as soon as the boat begins to slow the weight should be moved forward again. The daggerboard should be raised approximately 20 cm, this also helps to lift the bow from the water. The sail should be constantly trimmed as the boat is steered around the waves and up and down in the gust. Try to accelerate the boat and then take the speed low.

The leech should just twist slightly as pictured

Sit back as the boat accelerates

Reaching in strong winds

Sail Settings

Now that the boat is planing constantly the outhaul should be tighter as less lift is required and a tighter outhaul will create less drag. The kicker again can be eased more to create extra twist, but remember you are still trying to match a similar trim between the top and bottom of the sail. If overpowered the kicker can be eased to create more twist and to release power from the top of the sail. This also helps to reduce the chance of the boom tripping in the water. Leave the Cunningham off unless the reach is tight and you are overpowered.

Technique

Now you are more interested in top speed rather than acceleration of the boat. A looser kicker helps steering of the boat because there is less weather helm and the rudder movements have less effect on the rig. The bow should be kept high to help steering and prevent running into the back of waves so sit as far back as possible and raise the daggerboard 20 cm. Keep the boat trimmed on a constant heel by moving the body and sheeting simultaneously. If the boat is constantly heeling over and spinning into the wind try and sail the boat flatter and ease the kicker more.

Keep the boat flat

Sit as far back as possible

12 Sailing on a Reach

Gusts and Lulls

Sailing on a reach is pretty similar to running in that you want to spend as much time as possible in the gusts and the least amount of time in a lull. To achieve this you need to be sailing a lower course in the gusts and then a higher course in the lulls. This will increase the time spent in gusts and increase the boat's speed through the lulls getting the boat into the next gust faster. It is much quicker to sail the course that the wind takes you than to sail directly at the mark on the rhumb line.

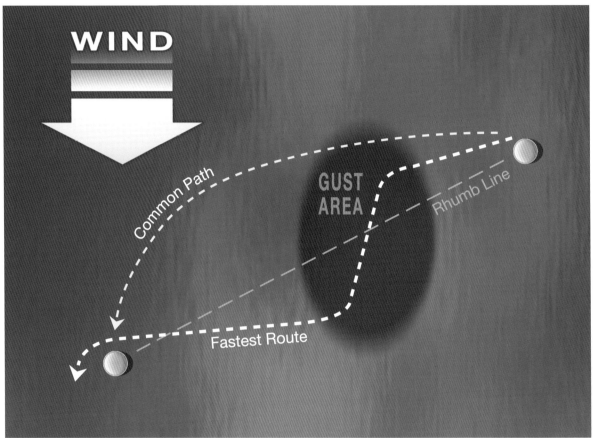

Taking the fast route on a reach

The body is positioned well aft with the daggerboard raised

Going Low Blast'n down
weymouth harbour in a strong gust

13 Laser Radial and 4.7

The Laser Radial

The Radial is a great alternative for lighter sailors or anybody that struggles with a full rig in stronger winds. The panel layout is different to the Laser Standard rig as the seams are laid in a radial cut from the clew, making the sail more sensitive to the Cunningham. The lower mast is shorter and softer than the standard rig allowing the rig to flex and release power more easily. In strong winds the Radial is much nicer to sail due to it being more balanced and less powerful. However it can be difficult to sail in lighter winds because there is less feel on the tiller, to compensate for this the boat may need to be sailed with slightly more leeward heel. In principle the techniques are very similar to a Laser 1 but because of the different sail shape and bottom mast the sail settings are slightly different. See the Radial Rig Settings Matrix for a more detailed breakdown (pages 108-109).

4.7 Rig

The 4.7 rig is much more similar to the full rig having the cloth orientation horizontal but using a pre-bent bottom section to balance the boat. It is a great boat for an introduction to Laser sailing and behaves in a similar way to the full rig. Due to the size of the rig the boat is very underpowered and will need to be sailed to optimise speed rather than height to windward. The 4.7 is difficult to accelerate and so it is very important to try to keep the boat moving as fast as possible in all conditions. The boat will probably be heavier on the helm so body movements will need to be exaggerated slightly to have any effect on the trim. The effect of the pre-bend in the lower mast will mean that less kicker tension is needed in lighter winds as the mast will not need to be bent to fit the sail. Be careful not to overtension the mainsheet, you don't really need to be block to block until you start hiking. The 4.7 rig should be set up slightly different to the full rig, see 4.7 rig settings matrix for a more detailed breakdown (pages 110-111).

13 Laser Radial and 4.7

Radial Rig Settings Matrix

| | Upwind | | | |
	Light	Medium	Strong	Light
Kicker	More than block to block, let off as wind increases	Block to block	More than block to block, increase tension as overpowered up to the point the boom does not rise when the mainsheet is eased	Loose to allow the leech to fan up to 30 cm either side of neutral
Cunningham	Tiny amount to remove the small creases	Just enough to remove the major diagonal creases, increase tension as you become overpowered	When completely overpowered pull on as hard as possible	Eased
Outhaul	20 cm deep at boom cleat, one hand	15 cm deep at boom cleat or a hand width	5-10 cm deep at boom cleat	Eased up to 25 cm
Mainsheet	Between 0-20 cm between the blocks ensuring the blocks are wide on the traveller	Block to block	When the sail is fully flattened and you are still overpowered play the main, being careful to avoid putting the boom end in the water	Allow the boom out as far as 90-110 degrees
Daggerboard	Down	Down	Down	Up 15 - 20 cm
Body Position	Forward by the daggerboard	Just behind the side deck cleat	Up to 15 cm behind the side deck cleat	Forward by the daggerboard
Trim	5-10 degrees leeward heel	Up to 5 degrees leeward heel	Flat as possible	10-20 degrees windward heel
Tips	Keep your head out of the boat, keep movements smooth and try and go block to block in the gusts	Hike as hard as you can, keep up all race	When the sail is fully flattened, play the main to keep the boat on its feet	Keep body movements to a minimum

	Downwind		Reaching		
	Medium	**Strong**	**Light**	**Medium**	**Strong**
	Loose enough to allow 30 cm of twist at the top of the sail	Loose enough to allow up to 30 degrees of twist	4-6 cm less than block to block	4 cm less than block to block	4-6 cm less than block to block
	Eased	Eased	Eased	Eased	Eased, but may be needed when overpowered on tight reaches
	Eased up to 25 cm	Eased up to 25 cm	15 cm deep	20 cm deep	10 -15 cm deep
	...ow the boom no further than 90 degrees	Allow the boom out to 75 - 85 degrees	Trim to the leeward tell tales	Trim to both tell tales	Trim to the leeward tell tales
	Up 15 - 20 cm	Up 15 - 20 cm	Up 15 - 20 cm	Up 15 - 20 cm	Up 15 - 20 cm
	Move back as the boat starts to accelerate and plane and then when the boat slows move your weight forward again.	Sit as far back as possible to lift the bow	Forward by the daggerboard	Move back as the boat starts to accelerate and plane and then when the boat slows move your weight forward again.	Sit as far back as possible to lift the bow
	...o to 10 degrees windward heel	Flat	5-10 degrees leeward heel	Up to 5 degrees leeward heel	Flat as possible
	Actively move around the boat to ...just to changes the conditions	Keep the main well inside 90 degrees and avoid dead running	Keep well forward	Steer and sheet to keep heel constant	Head up in the lulls and bear away in the gusts

13 Laser Radial

4.7 Rig Settings Matrix

	Upwind			Light
	Light	**Medium**	**Strong**	
Kicker	More than block to block, let off as wind increases	Block to block	More than block to block, increase tension as overpowered up to the point the boom does not rise when the mainsheet is eased	Loose to allow the leech to fan up to 20 cm either side of neutral
Cunningham	Eased	Just enough to remove the major diagonal creases, increase tension as the wind increases	On hard as possible	Eased
Outhaul	12 cm deep at boom cleat	8 cm deep at boom cleat or a hand width	8-4 cm deep at boom cleat	Eased up to 15 cm
Mainsheet	Between 0 - 20 cm between the blocks ensuring the blocks are wide on the traveller	Block to block	Try and keep block to block if possible	Allow the boom out as far as 90 -110 degrees
Daggerboard	Down	Down	Down	Up 15 - 20 cm
Body Position	Forward by the daggerboard	Just behind the side deck cleat	Flat as possible	Forward by the daggerboard
Trim	5-10 degrees leeward heel	Up to 5 degrees leeward heel	Flat	10-20 degrees windward heel
Tips	Keep your head out of the boat, keep movements smooth and try and go block to block in the gusts	Hike as hard as you can, keep up all race	Anticipate the gusts and let the main out if absolutely necessary	Keep body movements to a minimum

| Downwind | | Reaching | | |
Medium	Strong	Light	Medium	Strong
oose enough to w 20 cm of twist he top of the sail	Loose enough to allow up to 30 degrees of twist	2-3 cm less than block to block	3cms less than block to block	2-3 cms less than block to block
Eased	Eased	Eased	Eased	Eased, but may be needed when overpowered on tight reaches
Eased up to 15 cm	Eased up to 15 cm	15 cm deep	15 cm deep	10 -15 cm deep
ow the boom no urther than 90 degrees	Allow the boom out to 75 - 85 degress	Trim to the leeward tell tales	Trim to both tell tales	Trim to the leeward tell tales
Up 15 - 20 cm	Up 15 - 20 cm	Up 20 -25 cm	Up 20 -25 cm	Up 20 - 25 cm
ove back as the boat starts to elerate and plane d then when the slows move your ght forward again.	Sit as far back as possible to lift the bow	Forward by the daggerboard	Move back as the boat starts to accelerate and plane and then when the boat slows move your weight forward again.	Sit as far back as possible to lift the bow
to 10 degrees indward heel	Flat	5-10 degrees leeward heel	Up to 5 degrees leeward heel	Flat
ctively move und the boat to ust to changes the conditions	Keep the main well inside 90 degrees and avoid dead running	Keep well forward	Steer and sheet to keep heel constant	Head up in the lulls and bear away in the gusts

14 Fitness and Nutrition

Which rig?

To get the most out of sailing your Laser you need to be around the optimum weight and with a good basic level of fitness. If you are fitter and stronger it is easier to sail a larger rig than the recommended size for your given weight.

Fitness

How fit do you need to be?

This really depends on your aspirations and where you sail, and will vary greatly. When I was younger I remember Jim Saltonstall answering this very question to which he replied; "Fit enough to be sailing up the last beat of the last race as hard as you did up the first beat of the first race".

To get the most out of sailing any boat it is important to have a good level of basic fitness. Most sailors are unaware of how much their fitness affects their decision making and technique in the boat. A good level of fitness not only improves the physical aspects (for example hiking) but also their mental performance. When the body gets tired and fatigued it becomes difficult to concentrate and make the right decisions, thoughts usually wander from the boat speed, wind shifts and fleet to the pain going on in the legs. It is easy to blame a poor performance on a tactical error rather than addressing the true reasons – poor physical fitness caused the problems.

Everyone knows that the best way to train the muscles required for sailing is by spending as much time as possible on the water. An hour on the water trains the muscles you use better than three hours training on land and also helps develop your sailing skills. However, it is very difficult to spend the amount of training time required on the water so sailing should be supplemented with some off the water physical exercise. This training needs to be specific to the muscles that are used while sailing.

Optimum weights for each class

	Weight Range	Optimum Weight
Laser standard	74-86kg	78-83kg
Laser radial	58-75kg	65-70kg
Laser 4.7	40-58kg	50-54kg

This is not to say that if you are not within the weight band you should sail a different rig. A smaller rig is easier in heavy winds and a larger rig can be more exciting in lighter winds.

Identifying your weaknesses

You need to be honest with yourself and identify where your weaknesses are. Very rarely you will be out of breath due to physical activity while sailing but if you feel tired and struggle to concentrate after a few windy races then aerobic fitness training will be necessary. If your arms never tire or struggle when pulling the mainsheet or controls then you probably don't need to train your upper body in the gym, if they do then this is an area that can be improved. If your legs and abs tire and you are unable to hike as hard after the first beat then the legs and abs need to be made a priority, if they don't hurt at all you probably aren't trying hard enough!

The training areas to focus on are aerobic and strength training but not forgetting agility and core stability.

Aerobic training will help reduce fatigue and the efficiency of the body to recover.

Strength, core and agility training will help the body to function better in the boat and reduce the chance of injury.

Aerobic training

The best forms of aerobic training are rowing and cycling as these also help to train similar muscles in the body to those used while sailing and they are also low on impact. The Concept 2 rowing machine is probably the best way to train as it targets both the legs and the upper-body pulling muscles. If you prefer to be outside rather than in a gym especially on warmer days cycling is a good form of training. Cycling targets the legs and also concentrates the mind on staying on the bike and the environment - which can be a nice distraction to the physical exertion.

It is important to try and make the sessions enjoyable so that you will be more likely to keep doing them. If you are keen on your training it is a good idea to use a heart rate monitor as this will help you to monitor your training intensity and target your training.

A good programme to kick off your aerobic training is to do 2 x 40 minute sessions a week with a heart rate of around 75% of your maximum [if uncertain of your max heart rate it can be estimated by 220 – your age]. As you progress slowly increase the duration of the sessions by perhaps adding 5 minutes onto the duration every fortnight and also add a shorter more intense session of approx. 20 minutes at 85%.

Weight training

Weight training should be focused around pulling exercises for the upper body (similar to how muscles are used while sailing) and leg exercises to strengthen and increase the endurance of the legs. A good starter would be to use exercises that use your body weight as resistance to gain good form and technique before progressing on to using weights to increase the resistance.

A good starter programme would include the following exercises, 1 or 2 sessions per week:	
Walking lunges	10 each leg - 3 sets
Squats	15 reps - 2 sets
Assisted pull-ups	8 reps - 3 sets
Dumbbell single arm bent over row	10 reps each arm - 3 sets
Cable seated row	15 reps - 2 sets

When doing lots of specific training for sailing there is a danger that the body can become imbalanced which may lead to injury. This is only a real danger if weight training regularly. If this does happen then it will be necessary to work the opposite muscles such as the chest muscles on the upper-body, targeting these muscles as well will help to prevent any imbalances.

14 Fitness and Nutrition

Agility and Core Stability

Being mobile around the boat will not only help with technique but will also help prevent injury. Regular stretching will prevent the body from becoming stiff; it is good to incorporate a simple stretching routine after each physical exercise session whether it's shore based training or sailing. The muscles that are most prone to becoming tight and restricted due to sailing are the quads, hamstrings, calves and gluteals. Pay special attention to these muscles when stretching holding each stretch for over twenty seconds and repeat several times. Core stability is also vital to protect the back from being unnecessarily strained during hiking; it also improves your posture afloat and ashore. The best way to increase your core strength is to take part in Pilates classes (classes can be found locally at most decent sports centres or look on the Internet).

The key to fitness training is regime and fitting it into your everyday life, there is no point training every day for a week and then doing nothing for the rest of the month as this will do little to increase your fitness and only increases the chance of injury - training needs continuity to work. Make a realistic plan of what you are able to fit in each week around other commitments and stick to it.

A good level of shore based fitness will help the body to adapt to the sailing strains however you can be good in the gym and still feel sore after sailing if you haven't sailed for a while. Being fit in the boat is different to being fit onshore mainly because it is difficult to replicate sailing movements onshore.

Remember fitness is not everything, if you do not have the necessary sailing skills being fitter can mean that you can sail badly more comfortably for longer!

Nutrition

To sail and train well the body needs to be correctly fuelled and this will only come from what we eat and drink. A good balanced diet will help the body to recover from exercise and increase energy levels so that training and sailing on consecutive days is made easier. A balanced diet will include carbohydrate, fat, protein, minerals and vitamins but it is important to consume all the above in the right proportions. The easiest way to increase energy levels is by trying to reduce the amount of fat and increase the amount of carbohydrates.

Carbohydrates - there are two forms of carbohydrates, complex and simple. Complex carbohydrates are starch based and include foods such as pasta and rice and simple carbohydrates are sweet, sugar based. Foods high in simple carbohydrates include chocolate, sweets, cakes and other confectionery. Complex carbohydrates release energy slowly and simple carbohydrates give you a quick burst of energy. We need complex carbohydrates for slow releasing energy and this will help you go on longer, rather than the quick hit from simple carbohydrates which often means a dip or low after the hit. The complex carbohydrate foods include rice, pasta, potato and bread.

Proteins - are very important because they are responsible for growth and repair of the muscles. Good protein foods include milk, meat, fish and eggs. Beans and pulses also provide protein but the quality is not as good as the animal based foods.

Fat - intake should be kept to a minimum. Try to avoid fried and fatty foods, use olive oil in cooking but use sparingly. Oily fish such as mackerel, salmon, tuna and pilchards are great for providing essential fats.

Vitamins and minerals - make sure to eat enough vitamins and minerals which are found in fruit and vegetables. The recommended five portions a day is a great starting point.

If you are feeling very tired or under the weather supplement vitamin intake by taking a multi-vitamin tablet that can help boost the immune system and reduce the risk of illness. If using a multi-vitamin choose one that provides more than 100% of the Recommended Daily Allowance (RDA) for that nutrient.

Hydration

Keeping hydrated is probably the easiest way to boost performance on a long day. It is easy to neglect the body's need for water as it is often difficult to carry enough fluid on the boat. The body and mind will fatigue much quicker if the body gets dehydrated and this will reduce your performance. The best way to measure hydration is by monitoring the colour of your urine, the clearer the better. As soon as the urine is yellow it is too late and the body is already dehydrated, it is then hard to re-hydrate the body. Drinking water alone is not a good idea as vital salts in the body will be flushed out as you need to urinate more often. You can either add a pinch of salt to a squash drink or use a hydration drink. There are many on the market and now sold in large supermarkets as well sports shops. Look for a drink that provides about 6% carbohydrate (60g when made up to a litre) and about 20mmol of sodium. This will help to absorb the fluid rather than it just passing straight through the body. In warmer climates about a litre an hour needs to be consumed to reduce the risk of dehydration.

15 Clothing

The type of clothing worn while sailing is important to your performance. If you are comfortable, warm and unrestricted you can manoeuvre around the boat easily, concentrate and remain focused.

Hikers

The main clothing performance gain in Laser sailing comes from wearing hiking shorts. When hiking in a neoprene wetsuit or ordinary shorts the thighs squash over the gunwale which is uncomfortable and restricts blood flow through the legs. Hiking shorts are designed to spread the pressure on the back of the legs when they are pressed against the deck and raise up the sailor slightly. Battens or pads are attached to the leg of the neoprene shorts helping spread the pressure along the leg, thus increasing the blood flow through the legs.

The key to a good pair of hikers is fit and batten or pad position. The wetsuit needs to fit well so that the battens don't move around the leg while sailing. The battens and pads also need to be large enough and in a position to spread the load if you are hiking either flat out with the side of the deck just above the back of the knee or just perched hiking with the deck closer to your bottom.

Year round hikers

Summer Clothing

In the summer it is easy to keep mobile and unrestricted by wearing thin 3mm hiking pants with a Lycra top to help keep the body cool and protected from the sun.

Winter Clothing

In colder weather it is much harder to keep warm without restricting the body's movement. I find that the best compromise is wearing neopene hiking shorts on the lower body with several thermals or even a fleece under a good quality dry top which will keep the thermals dry and you warm with minimal restriction to the upper body, or a long-john style of hiking shorts with a good quality wetsuit worn over thermals. An alternative is a 5mm wetsuit or dry suit with a pair of hiking shorts over the top but this can be quite restrictive. A woolly hat is important in the cold as most heat loss occurs from the head. A pair of neoprene wet socks worn under boots can help keep the feet warm and also provide extra padding for hiking.

Buoyancy aids

Buoyancy aids are compulsory when racing and even when just cruising about they should be worn at all times. Not as large and restricting as conventional life jackets they come in several designs and many sizes. A good tight fitting jacket designed specifically for dinghy sailing is preferable with minimal zips and fastenings as these inevitably get caught in something when sailing. The jacket should hug the body reducing the risk of it getting caught when passing beneath the boom. A Lycra vest or rash top can be worn over the life jacket to prevent it getting caught up.

Spray top or dry top?

The decision to wear a spray or dry top is a personal thing. For me it usually depends on how windy or cold it is. In warmer weather a spray top is preferred as the seals at the neck and wrist are more comfortable but in cold and windy conditions a good dry top will keep the thermals underneath dry and you warm. Some people find the latex seals irritating and uncomfortable but by using talcum powder and cutting the seal to the correct size for you they are a good alternative to wearing a spray top.

Spray top

Dry top

Boots

Boots are essential to provide support and protection to the feet. They should be a good fit helping support the ankle when hiking, and providing additional padding between the foot and the toe strap. The sole of the boot is important for grip on the cockpit floor and sides when manoeuvring. I like to wear boots with ridges on the top. The ridges help to grip the strap and stop the feet sliding around when moving the upper body whilst hiking.

Caps

I like to wear a cap in all conditions as it not only helps vision in sunny conditions but can also protect the face from spray and rain.

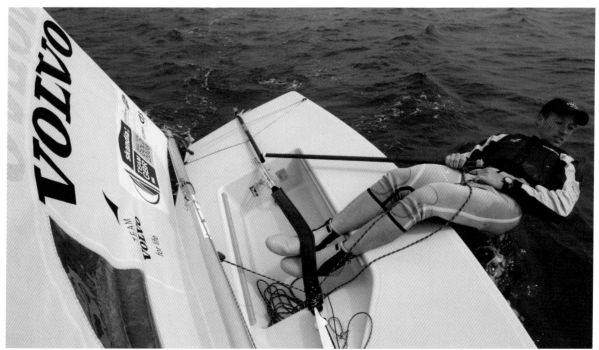

A good pair of boots and hiking shorts will make hiking much more comfortable

16 Starting

Laser racing is generally very tight because there is little difference in boat speed due to the one-design nature of the class, this makes it very difficult to have an edge making starting one of the most important aspects of the race. Starting is also one of the most difficult aspects of sailing to become consistent at, due to there being so many external factors and you will be closer to all your competitors than at any other stage of the race.

Starting can make a difference of between 10–90 percent of doing well in a race. The percentage depends on the course and conditions. To make a good start you need to make the right decisions in your preparation.

Pre Start checks

You should aim at getting out to the racecourse with a minimum of 30 minutes to the start; this allows time to become comfortable with the conditions and set up the rig, take note of any wind patterns either direction or strength. Get a feel for any current in the starting area, this will influence the approach. Your plan for the start will be easier to make once these factors have been considered.

Choosing where to start

If there is no definite strategy for the beat, you want to start at the favoured end, the one most upwind and nearest to the windward mark. The easiest way to do this is by sailing down the line from one end and then luffing and sitting head to wind. The end of the line that the bow of the boat is pointing nearest to is the favoured end. Once the favoured end has been chosen decide how heavily the end is biased and how close to that end you need to be. If the line is heavily biased it is really important to be as close to that end as possible. If the bias is only slight this is less important.

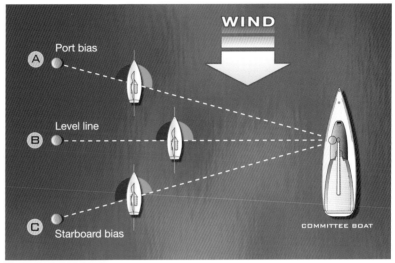

Picking the favoured end

Transits

The next thing to do is get a transit; this will help us to judge where the line is and your position relative to the line. Normally this is easier to do looking through the port end of the line from the starboard end; however it can be done the other way and is sometimes useful if the former is unavailable. To gain a transit sit by the starboard end of the line and sight the pin end, look beyond the pin end for something distinctive and inline. This is an exact transit which is hard to view when queuing up pre-start but is used to judge where you are on the line at start time. Another safe transit is needed to help the approach to the start. This is taken from behind the line at the starboard end; if this is from two boat lengths behind the line then you will only be one boat length behind the line in the middle of the line on this transit. In the case illustrated below there are two trees, be careful not to get confused between the two. If you are going to be approaching from a long way back get a third safer transit such as the building below, it is good to note any objects on the shore between the transits to help judge the speed of change when approaching the line. Is the line approaching quickly or slowly?

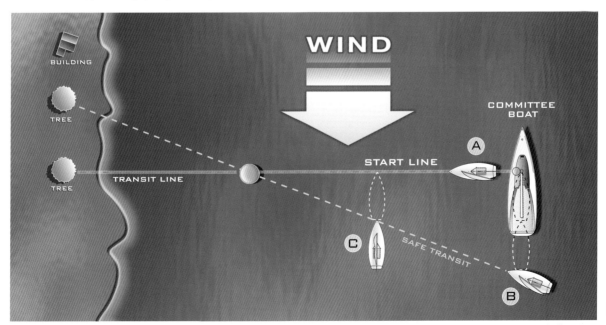

If you are unable to get a good transit then do not start in the middle of the line because there is every chance that you will be nowhere near the line or miles over at start time

16 Starting

Approach

It is important to judge the correct speed of approach to the line, if you approach too late it will be difficult to find a space, too soon and you are vulnerable to other boats coming in below. Be alert and fully focused as things can change quickly in the run up to the start. In the last 30 seconds, try and keep level with boats around, so you don't drop out of the pack because it is difficult to get back in to the front row. In the final 15–20 seconds it is crucial to create a gap to leeward to accelerate into at start time. If you're in doubt about being over the line try and stay well covered, if you think you're going to be over, bail out as soon as possible as a bad start is much better than a no start due to an OCS (on course side penalty).

Accelerating at the start

Getting off the line is crucial. It is possible to do all the pre-start perfectly and then not get off the line. This last bit is all down to timing and acceleration. Use your boat handling skills to create a gap to accelerate into. Timing is the key to a good start and you need to have maximum concentration. The amount of time you require to create a gap and then accelerate varies on the wind speed and sea state. At start time the boat needs to be set up for the first beat except that the kicker is loose, stopping the boat from going forward when the mainsheet is out. It is also much easier to control and steer the boat. Pull on the kicker and accelerate the boat to hit the line at full speed on the gun.

The seconds after the gun are vital, it is all about competing against the boats around you so 100% of your concentration should be on boat speed, once you have popped out from your group it is time to start looking around and executing your first beat plan. See Chapter 6 Racing Manoeuvres: Acceleration.

Port end start on a port biased line

It is important to remember that due to the wind angle it takes longer to approach the line on starboard tack than if the line is unbiased. This needs to be taken into consideration when thinking about acceleration, time and distance. On heavily biased lines it is easy to become stranded behind the line with not enough time to reach the line at the gun. You also need to take into account what the pin end is, is it a boat or a buoy and how much mooring line is to windward of it. It is vital to avoid a raft at the pin. This is common when boats that are not making the pin luff or even tack to make it round. If you can pre-empt this happening it is much better to bail out early and give yourself time to find a new place further up the line. You should try and have a good understanding of the rules: infringements are common as boats fail to get around the pin.

On a long start line it is common for there to be a 'sag'

Mid line start on a level line

On most starts there is nearly always line sag where boats in the middle of the line sometimes start as far away as three boat lengths from the line. It is crucial to have confidence in a good transit. Several transits are needed ranging from a few boat lengths behind the line to on the line. This helps to judge the time and distance by the rate of change between the transits. Another method to use is to point the bow at the pin end, hold the tiller centred and look down the tiller towards the starboard end. If the extension of this line is two boat lengths behind the Committee Boat then you will be one length behind the line in the centre of it. The key to a good mid-line start is knowing where the line is and not to give this away to the other boats. If you sit right on the line you are showing the other boats where the line is and they will advance with you. You should stay with the group as long as possible, giving you the opportunity to accelerate for the start really early, starting well in front of the boats around you but on the line making a great start. Only start in the middle of the line when you are really confident with your transits.

Starboard end start on a starboard biased line

On starboard tack due to the wind angle you approach the line much quicker than you would on a level line so you need to be aware of this when checking your time and distance. The start boat may also affect matters, if the boat is large it may cause a wind shadow. When trying to win the starboard end you have to be there early, otherwise you can get forced to the wrong side of the committee boat, or even end up starting on the second or third row.

Strategy

You need when planning your starting strategy to consider the quality of the fleet and its make up. The lower the quality of the fleet the easier it will be to win the favoured end. The make up of the fleet can have a huge effect on your starting strategy. In handicap racing the speed and manoeuvrability of boats can be very different, you don't want to start next to a faster boat and then post start immediately be in dirty air. When you race consistently in a fleet it pays to discover what level and style of sailors your competitors are, and how they sail their boats. For instance, if you generally sail your boat high upwind and pinch, you do not want to start below somebody who sails their boat more freely than you. Knowledge of all your competitors and their sailing characteristics especially of those you have on either side of you at start time will help determine how you should sail off the start. The type of start situation will also have implications on strategy, a black flag, Z flag or round the ends start will need a very different approach to a normal start.

Risk Management

One of the biggest decisions you face when starting is how far am I willing to push the line before I risk being over. This is a complicated decision and is determined by many factors.

- How important is this race?
- Are you strong or weak in these conditions?
- What is the potential for position change?

If the conditions are stable meaning that there are fewer overtaking opportunities and the line is heavily biased, then a higher risk should be taken at the start than in conditions that are shifty and allow more overtaking opportunities with a level start line. Towards the end of the regatta it is also worth considering what results you need in order to achieve your goal, do you need to take any risks?

17 Compass Work

I have resisted for years using a compass because I started sailing on inland locations and on short courses. I used the angles of other boats, transits on the shore and the angles of small waves to navigate around wind shifts, however this is not easy and takes years of practice. A compass helps when making decisions because there is an actual true figure rather than an estimate of an angle therefore removing any guesswork.

Standard scale 0-360

Tactical compass scale

There are two types of compass you can use: one has a tactical scale of 0-19 and the other a regular scale of 0–360.

Tactical compass - the scale divides 360 degrees into 20 units, marked 0 to 19, each mark corresponding to 18 degrees.

The viewing lubber lines give the sailor a similar number to remember on each upwind tack.

For a northerly wind (at 0 degrees) the helmsman reads 0 on the tactical scale on the starboard lubber line and given a tacking angle of 80 degrees the viewer sees 10 on the port lubber line making the number easier to remember.

Standard scale compass - the advantage of using a standard scale is that the numbers can easily be related back to the true wind direction. The number is an actual angle not a fraction of one.

There are several compass designs available; I prefer a vertical facing compass like the Silva 103r which has a 360 degree graduation rather than a tactical scale. The compass can be attached to the boat using a number of different brackets and needs to be secure on the deck as small movements could disguise changes in boat tracking angles.

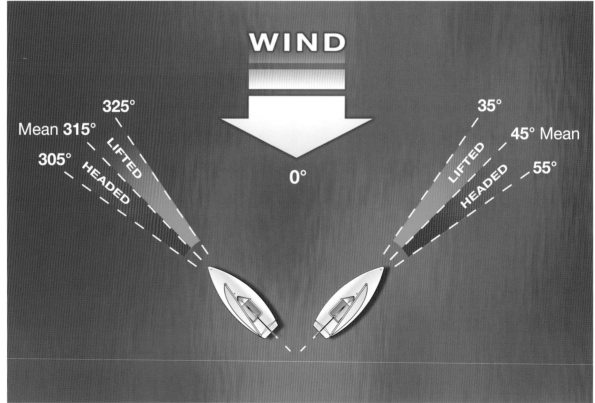

Illustration A

The compass is used while sailing to windward by reading the numbers on the windward lubber lines and using the line in the middle of the compass to take actual headings. A compass can be a very useful tool for spotting wind shifts, bends and checking the line bias especially when sailing offshore or with low visibility. Before the race starts the compass is used to track the wind to establish any patterns and relate this to the forecast. You should take wind readings regularly by pointing the bow head to wind and reading the direction.

The most accurate way to check the line bias is by using a compass. Sit at the starboard end of the line and pointing the bow at the port end and sailing towards it, take the bearing of the line. If the wind direction is at 90 degrees to the line bearing then the line is square. If less than 90 degrees the port end is favoured and more than 90 degrees the starboard end is favoured (see illustration B).

This method gives an accurate reading of how much bias is on the line and therefore how critical it is to be at the favoured end. A bias of only 5 degrees is pretty insignificant, if the bias is 20 degrees then it is going to be critical to be at the favoured end.

Once racing and sailing upwind the compass is now used to spot wind shifts. If the numbers are rising when sailing on starboard then you are being lifted and should stay on this tack. If the numbers are decreasing then you are being headed and should therefore look to tack.

The reverse happens when on port, if the numbers decrease you are headed and if they increase lifted.

You should try and remember the average numbers for each tack as this will help to decide whether you are lifted or headed when you round the leeward mark helping to decide whether to tack or stay on (see illustration A).

The final advantage of using a compass is when the course is changed due to a wind shift. It is important to use the compass to sight the new windward mark from the bearing from the race committee boat and establish its position relative to the old one.

If you generally sail on land locked waters and are thinking of using a compass for sailing at an open sea venue it is a good idea to practise using the compass before you get there to become familiar with it.

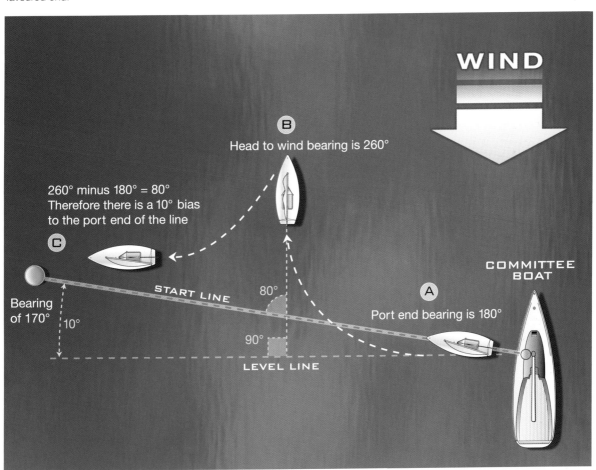

Illustration B

18 Regatta Preparation

One of the great things about sailing is that no two regattas are the same because there are different conditions and local effects. It is important to prepare well for a regatta because good preparation will have a large influence on success. Good preparation increases confidence and cuts down the number of surprises that may distract your focus.

It is important to plan in advance

- When to arrive
- Who to train with
- Where to stay
- Which equipment to use (using new untested gear is never a good idea)
- Acquire a chart to review the wind and tides expected
- Ask people who have sailed there in the past

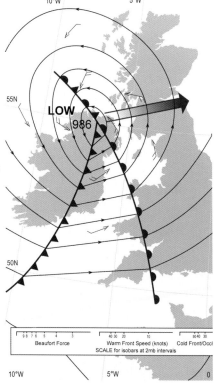

When planning for an event try to get everything arranged before you leave so that when you arrive you can concentrate on sailing. All too often people arrive at the venue not knowing where to stay and having to do boat work before they are able to get out sailing.

Try to arrive at the venue a few days before the regatta starts so that you have time to settle in and get to know your surroundings, Sail on the race course and recognise any local effects on the wind, tide and sea state, get comfortable with the venue so that nothing feels too strange. Pre-event training should be about getting used to sailing in a different venue.

- Make sure that your boat handling is sharp and your sail settings are correct for the conditions.
- Try not to alter technique or equipment just before an event, this can be distracting.
- It is very easy to over-train prior to a big event by spending long hours on the water and this can lead to the danger of becoming stale.
- Make sure you have time to relax and unwind and be careful not to wear your self out before the event starts.
- You need the hunger and confidence to sail well.

Local Knowledge

Each venue has its own characteristics and local effects and it's a good idea beforehand to get a chart of the racing area and the tide times. By looking at the chart you can identify any possible effect the local topography may have on the race course and identify features such as channel marks etc. You can then identify where you are on the water in relation to the chart. Ideally this should be done before you arrive at the venue but the best way to gain the most relevant and valuable information is by sailing in the racing area.

Make a note after each sail on the weather conditions and any trends that you found. It is a good idea to ask locals for their knowledge and ideas - but be careful with this information, it is not always reliable or relevant. Always make sure the

information source is reliable. Check out any theories during the practice sessions and make a decision on whether it is useful and relevant. Only use information that you feel confident with, use factual information and go with what you see on the day.

An accurate daily weather forecast is important to help identify any changes that may occur during the day so you can be prepared and in the right mind set; whether it's just to decide what clothes you take on the water or what time a weather front might pass. There are several web sites that can be used such as the BBC and Wind Guru. Check each morning during training and decide how useful and accurate it has been, this will help you to decide how useful this information will be during the regatta.

18 Regatta Preparation

Physical Preparation

Before the regatta starts you need to be physically well prepared. Assuming you have a good sailing fitness for the boat, the main thing is to stay healthy and avoid the risk of injury. It is so easy the day before the regatta to go and play football and twist your ankle or have a crash on a mountain bike, it's been done before! It is most important to have enough sleep and to eat a good diet to help the body build and recover. Breakfast is important and should contain a high level of carbohydrates; cereals, toast and orange juice are good examples. While training and racing on the water it is hard to consume enough food at the right time. A carbohydrate drink is a good supplement to energy bars and sandwiches. This will help to increase liquid and carbohydrate intake helping to keep energy levels high. Also important is to keep well hydrated, this aids recovery, increases performance and helps maintain concentration. Evening meals should be rich in carbohydrates, pastas, rice and potatoes also some proteins, try to keep fat intake low. Eating the recommended intake of vitamins and minerals will help to keep the body healthy. If the body has worked hard then energy stores deplete each day unless sufficient food and drink have been consumed. It's a good idea to have an easy (lazy!) day before the regatta, sail if you need to sail but I suggest just an hour on the water so you have time to relax and make the final checks to the boat.

Boat Preparation

Before the regatta starts your boat should be as well prepared as your body and if possible any major boatwork should be done before arriving at the venue leaving just a final "check and tickle" the day before the start. Boat preparation does not win regattas but regattas can be lost if equipment fails.

Spars

Wash the spars and make sure they are clean and smooth so that the sail can slide easily up and down the mast. The end of the boom where the clew strap slides should either be polished or sprayed with Mc lube or similar. The fittings need to be checked for cracks and wear especially around the rivets as this is where the spars are most likely to break. If there are any cracks discard the mast and use another one. Finally check that the mast collars have a tight fit, if necessary tape around the top mast plugs.

Finishing the foils

The foils need to be smooth to create a good surface for water to flow over because this is where the lift is created. The foils should be checked for deep scratches and dents, any scratches or dents should be sanded and filled to make the board smooth. It is a good idea to lightly sand the foils with 1000 grade sandpaper to remove any imperfections. I then like to polish the rudder which helps keep the blade cleaner for longer, a sanded finish gets dirty as particles stick to the surface. Polishing the daggerboard makes the board move up and down easily when sailing, but when sailing in waves the board becomes prone to popping up slightly while sailing upwind which is not good! It can also make it very difficult to climb onto and hold the daggerboard if you were to capsize so it is best to leave this with a matt finish. If the foils are humming then there is a problem with the finish and it is usually the trailing edge. Sand the trailing edge of the foils using a sanding block and paper to remove any imperfections. Check that the rudder when pushed fully down achieves an angle of 78 degrees, if this angle is less then more weather helm may be encountered.

Hull

The hull should be smooth and have a good finish to reduce the amount of drag being created as it passes through the water. The best finish is a simple wash of the boat to remove any dirt or stains and then if required a polish. Polishing the boat also helps to keep the boat clean as dirt is less likely to stick to the hull when sailing in and out of polluted harbours etc. If the boat has any small scratches sand these out, any large deep scratches can be filled with gel coat and then sanded fair to the hull.

Tape the mast collars for a tight fit

Sand and polish the foils

Bailer

The bailer should be checked so that it moves up and down smoothly and that no weed or other garbage is trapped. This can be done by turning the boat upside down and peering through the bailer. If the bailer doesn't move smoothly the internal rubber bailer bands may need replacing, to do this you need to remove the bailer and replace with new bailer bands or an alternative such as rubber bands. Several of the top sailors in the world use either tape to fair in the front of the bailer or even a sticker to fair in the whole bailer.

Tape can be used to fair the front of the bailer

Basic spares

It's a good idea to organise and keep handy a basic tool kit so that you are prepared if anything should break, going around borrowing tape and tools is a waste of time and can make you unpopular in the boat park.

The night before the regatta it is a good idea to have read the sailing instructions, pack your bags for the morning checking you have all your sailing kit. Prepare drinks and on water snacks so everything is ready for the big day.

Finally and most importantly go out and enjoy the regatta.

Fittings

Deck fittings over time may become loose, so check the screws are taut and not spinning.

Gudgeons - Special attention should be given when checking the gudgeons, take care not to overtighten these screws as it could bend the plastic. If the gudgeons are worn they can either be replaced or turned upside down. All the deck fittings should be checked for wear and signs of cracking.

Friction pad - Needs to be adjusted or replaced before a regatta so that the daggerboard is held tight in place to stop the board slipping up or down while racing.

Blocks - Over time blocks can wear and seize especially if sailing from a sandy beach. All the blocks should be checked so that they are running smoothly. Check that the ropes are not worn at any turning or chafing points and tape or burn the ends of ropes to prevent them from fraying. Blocks and ropes could also be lubricated with a dry lubricant such as Mc lube or equivalent to make the controls more efficient.

A basic tool kit should consist of

- Drill
- Rivet gun
- Rivets
- Knife
- Screwdrivers

- Sandpaper
- Marine filler
- Electrical tape
- Spare blocks and rope

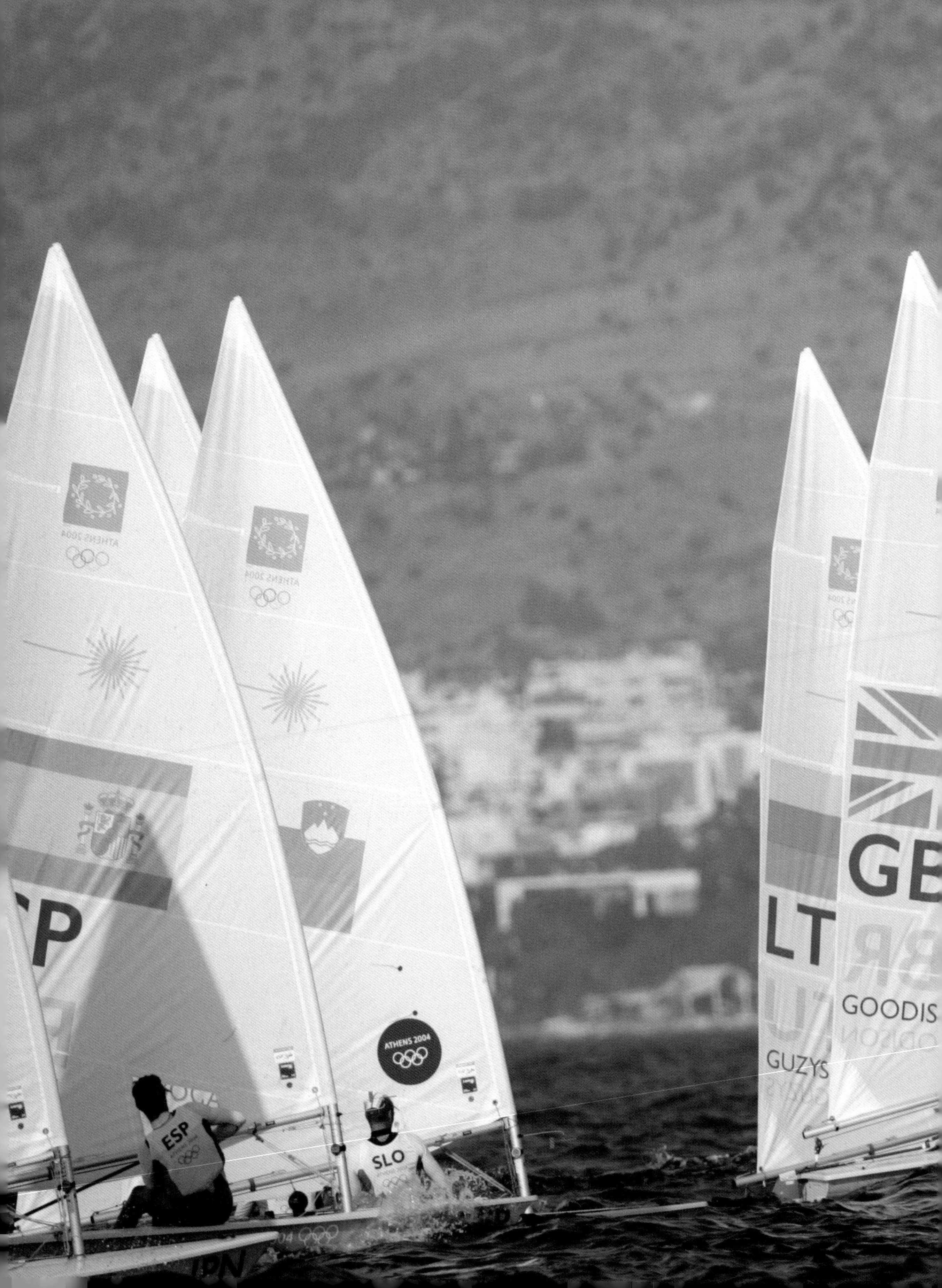
ATHENS 2004
ESP
SLO
LT
GUZYS
GB
GOODIS

19 Goal Setting

To help structure your development and learning it is a good idea to work out where in your sailing performance you want to be; this will enable you to plan a strategy of how to work out how you are going to reach that goal. There are many methods of goal setting to help your training and progress. I believe in general that people make their goal setting too complicated and impractical to use and update regularly. It is a good idea to get your coach or someone who knows your sailing well to help you with your goals which should be written down and used for future reference.

Dream Goal

Have something which you would love to achieve in your sailing, this can be something that is unlikely to happen for a long time. At the time you write it down it may look unrealistic, but it will help you define what your more immediate outcome goals are and then, hopefully, in the future it will become an outcome goal itself.

Outcome Goal

The next thing to do is write down your outcome goal. It is a good idea to only set one of these per season, even though there is likely to be more than one event where you want to get a good result (these extra events can become process goals towards your outcome goal). Having one goal will help with visualisation, which in turn helps you to peak at the right time.

Process Goals

These can be thought of as the here and now goals. Sailors will often use the dartboard illustration (see page 132) to map out their process goals. The goals must be SMART (Specific, Measurable, Attainable, Realistic and Time phased) because all your process goals, which dictate your training, will stem from this goal. A common mistake is not to use it in conjunction with the outcome goal, without which the scores have little relevance. If you take a score of 10 as where you need to be to attain your outcome goal it gives you a measure of how much work you have to do in each highlighted area. For example you might not be very good at light wind tacks, but you know the venue for your outcome goal is likely to have light winds, so although you are only a 6 in terms of ability, it is good enough for your outcome goal to be a 10. The aspect of your sailing that you choose to put in each segment is up to you. You could have one dartboard with general areas and another with more specific details of one of the highlighted areas. Once you have highlighted the areas of concern, write down ideas of how you can improve. This will give direction to your training days because you will know what you want to get out of each day. It will also help you to decide how much training to do and how many events to attend. You will probably find that, at first, your process goals are not very detailed, but once you start training in that aspect you are able to amend them and make the process goals more specific.

Monitoring

Once you have highlighted your process goals, it is essential to keep monitoring them. Each time you go sailing write down what you want to achieve and how you are going to do it and after sailing write down what you have achieved and what you need to do next time in similar conditions. The notes will help commit things to memory and help prevent being distracted into other areas.

Every month review your training and fill in another dartboard illustration to check your progress with your process goals. If you have not improved in certain areas, have a look through your training notes and see if you have neglected those areas or have not been doing the correct exercises. This is likely to instigate more goal setting and stimulate ideas on how to move closer to achieving the outcome goal.

19   Goal Setting

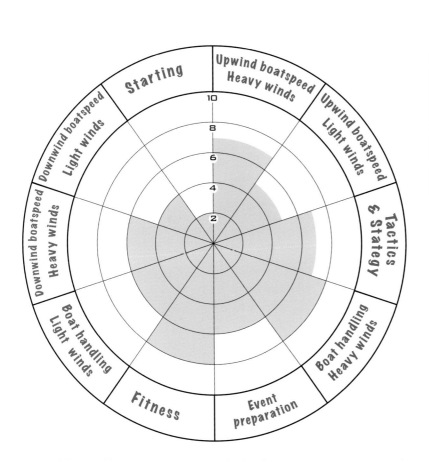

General Evaluation

This dartboard shows that the area of 'starting' needs the most work to achieve the outcome goal, whilst 'Upwind boatspeed in heavy winds' needs the least amount of work.

Area of Specific Evaluation - Starting

This dartboard takes a closer look at areas of starting and shows that training should be focused on high risk and light wind starting.

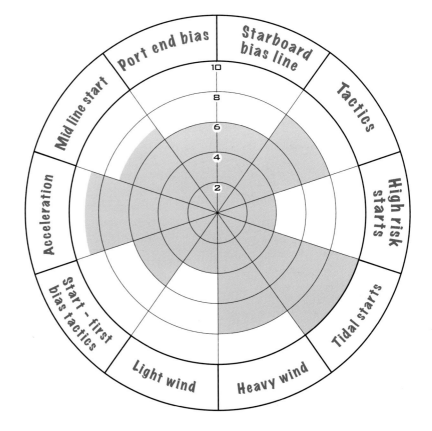

The following is a rough guide to help keep the boat in good condition and to reduce the risk of causing damage.

Trolley

The best way to keep the hull in good condition is to have a well padded trolley. It's important for the trolley to support the boat to avoid scratches and damage to the hull. A gunwale hung trolley is best due to no pressure being placed through the underside of the hull. It is best to use foam lagging to pad the trolley because it will not absorb water. Pad the trolley at the bow to stop the black marks caused by the trolley's rubber pads but don't pad between the gunwale hung supports, as the boat will permanently sit on this and not be supported under the gunwale.

Foils

These can be affected by the sun and heat. In hot climates keep the foils in the shade and out of extremely hot places, preferably laid on a flat surface. I have seen a daggerboard melt around a tiller on a sunny day in Athens when the board was left lying on top of the tiller. To straighten the board I poured boiling water over the trailing edge to re-heat the board and deflected the trailing edge the opposite way before cooling with cold water, this helped to straighten the board back to its original shape. I have also seen hair straighteners used to fix the problem!

Masts

A topmast should be straightened if it has bent while sailing. If there is only a slight bend the mast can simply be rotated through 180 degrees before the next sail. This however is not advised if the mast is severely bent or the wind is over 12 knots for the next sail. If the wind is over 12 knots then the rivet should always be in line with the gooseneck keeping it in compression. For straightening the mast see The Laser: Spars (page 20).

Removing scratches from the hull

Scratches can be removed in two ways, small scratches can simply be removed by running a sharp razor blade over the scratched area until the scratch is removed, deeper scratches by using a sanding block and sandpaper. The best way of knowing how much to sand the hull is by colouring over the scratched area with a marker pen. Simply use a permanent marker and colour over the scratched area (see picture 1). Ideally start wet and drying with 800 grade sandpaper but a deeper scratch may require starting with a coarser grade. Use a sanding block to keep the area that is being sanded flat with the surrounding area (see picture 2). As you sand, the scratches will become visible as black lines (see picture 3). As the lines become fainter switch to 1000 grade paper and as soon as the pen marks disappear stop sanding. The area can then be polished to finish. If the scratch is through the gel coat into the fibreglass it will need to be filled with gel coat and then sanded flush with the hull.

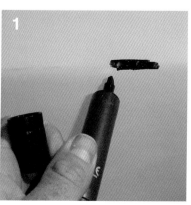

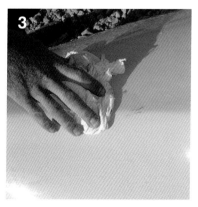

Towing on the water

When towing the boat on the water behind a RIB or something similar, the tow rope should be attached around the lower mast just above the deck. This will help to spread the load through the boat and is more secure than tying to the bow eye or other fittings. If a string of boats are towed behind, then the towlines can be tied to the tow line not the boat (see photo 4). This means your boat only takes the weight of itself with the towlines taking the weight of all the boats behind.

Only tie one line around each mast when towing more than one boat

Transport

There are several ways of transporting a Laser; either by towing the boat on a trailer or on the roof of the car. It is probably best to put the boat on the roof of a car as poor suspension on trailers causes a lot of strain throughout the boat. Make sure that the boat is secured using webbing straps as this helps to spread the load, remember tight ropes can leave imprints on the hull if over-tightened. Remember to carry a spare wheel when trailing the boat and to check that the lighting board is working properly before you set off.

21 Training Exercise 1

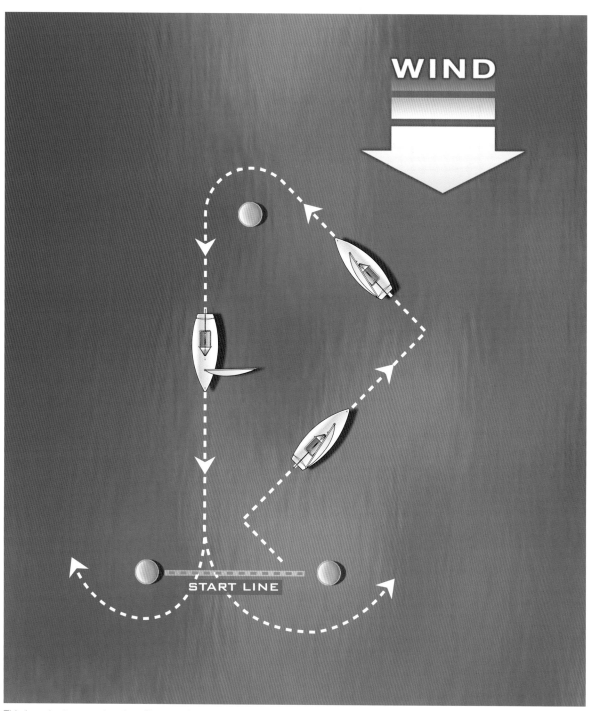

WIND

START LINE

This is a short course boathandling exercise, concentrate specifically on mark roundings both windward and leeward. You may stop after each lap to prioritise starting or do several laps for general boathandling.

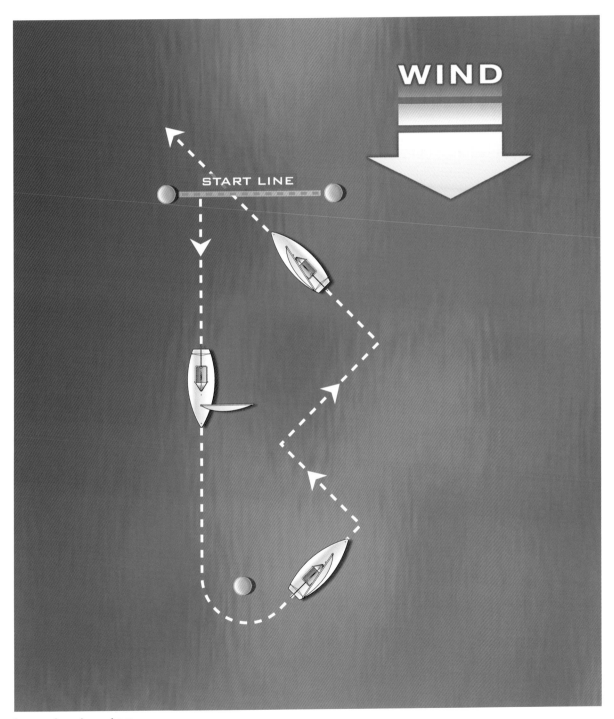

Leeward mark mayhem

When used with several boats there is more pressure to get inside line. Start with one or two boats and gradually increase with confidence.

21 Training Exercise 3

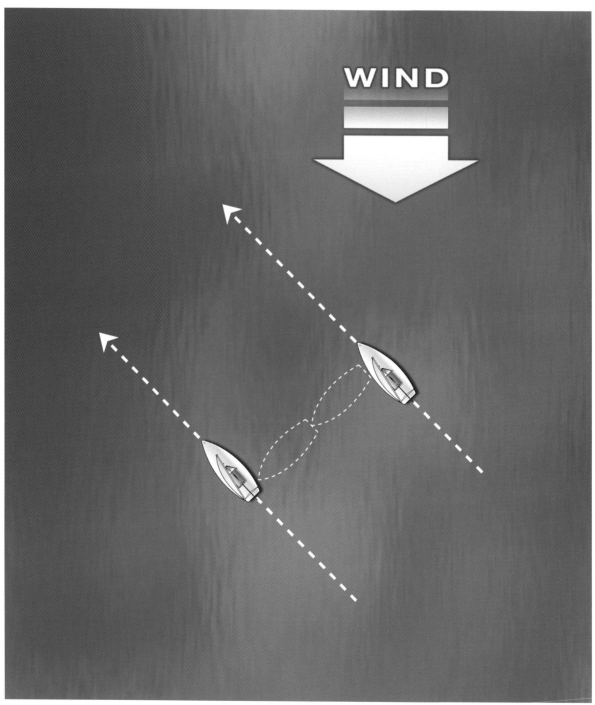

Upwind Tuning
Sail upwind together to test speed if one boat gets advanced stop and restart. The closer the boats the more difficult it will be for the windward boat.

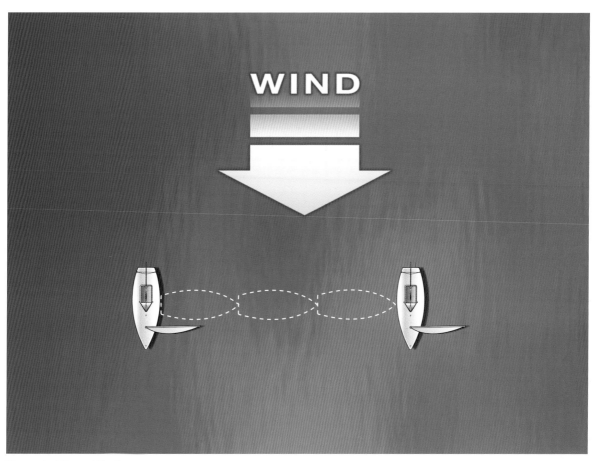

Downwind Speed Testing

Start side by side and bear away together, when one boat gains a lead stop and start again.

21 Training Exercise 5

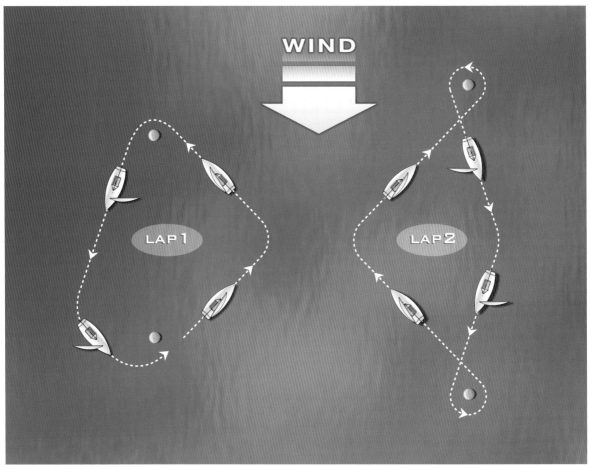

This exercise is great for boathandling combining both windward and leeward mark roundings, tacking and gybing. The shorter the course the more demanding the exercise.

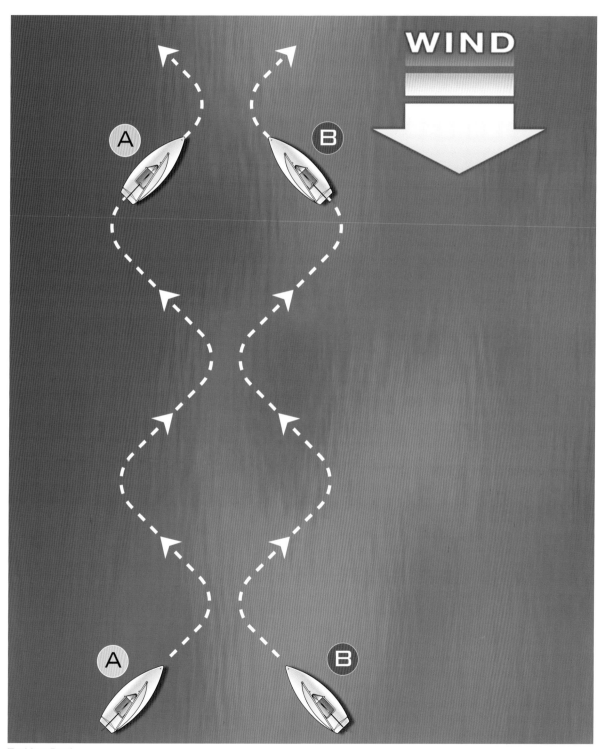

Tacking Dual

Sail at each other, as you come together tack, then sail and tack again. The less time between tacks the harder the exercise. Stop if one boat gets in front.

'Laser Sailing has given me some amazing experiences and I have met some incredible friends. I hope you have fun developing your skills and achieve your ambitions whether that's an Olympic medal or a club race win.'

Paul Goodison

Glossary

Air block	Pulley through which control lines pass, secured by rope
Battens	Sail stiffeners inserted into pockets
Becket	Fitting for securing ropes
Block	Pulley through which control lines pass
Boom eye	Strengthened hole in sail used to attach it to rear end of boom
Bouncing	Body movement to windward when hiking
Bowline	Knot
Cleat	Deck fitting for attaching ropes
Clew	Lower rear corner of sail
Clew tie	Used to attach lower rear corner of sail to boom
Control lines	Rope systems for controlling boom and sails
Cunningham	A sail's luff tension control (downhaul)
Daggerboard	Lifting keel
Drag	Forces acting to slow down boat
Fairlead	Deck fitting which ropes pass through
Foils	Daggerboard and rudder
Gooseneck	Fitting where boom attaches to mast
Gudgeons	Rudder pivot bearings
Gunwale	Top edge of hull
Gybing	Changing direction when sailing downwind
Heel angle	Angle at which boat leans
Hikers	Reinforced shorts for hiking
Hiking	Leaning out to counter balance forces on sail
In irons	When boat loses way between tacks
Kicker	(kicking strap) Control pulling boom downwards
Leech	Trailing edge of sail
Leeward	Downwind direction
Leeway angle	Difference between directions boat is travelling and pointing
Lift	Force acting on sail and foils to power boat forward
Line bias	Angle at which start line differs from being square to wind
Lubber lines	Marker lines on compass showing boat's direction
Luff tension	Tightness in part of sail attached to mast
Luffing	Altering course towards wind
Mainsheet	Main control rope for sail
Mast step	Fitting in hull for locating mast
OCS	On Course Side of the start line (penalty before start of race)
Outhaul	Rope system for horizontally tensioning sail
Pintles	Rudder pivot pins
Planing	Where hull reaches sufficient speed to travel on surface of water
Reaching	Sailing between beating and running
Rhumb line	Direct line between marks
Rudder stock	Part of rudder assembly which hinges on transom

Glossary

Running	Sailing with the wind behind
Sail camber	Sail depth
Sail draft	Area of most fullness
720	Penalty turn
Sheeting	Pulling or easing control lines
Spars	Boom and mast
Tacking	Sailing to windward by using a zig-zag course
Tell tales	Pieces of material attached to sail to indicate wind flow
Tiller	Steering arm attached to rudder
Toe strap	Strap under which feet are placed when hiking
Transit	Position judged by lining up two objects
Transom	Rear of hull

Traveller	Rope across stern controlling movement of boom via control lines
Trim	Correctly balancing boat, e.g. by finding best body position
Vang	See Kicker
vmg	Velocity made good – speed made towards or away from the wind, rather than speed through the water
Windward	Towards the direction wind is blowing from

Training Notes

Training Notes

Training Notes

Training Notes

Index

Index

Index

RYA *Membership*

Promoting and Protecting Boating
www.rya.org.uk

RYA Membership
Promoting and Protecting Boating

The RYA is the national organisation which represents the interests of everyone who goes boating for pleasure.

The greater the membership, the louder our voice when it comes to protecting members' interests.

Apply for membership today, and support the RYA, to help the RYA support you.

Benefits of Membership

- Special members' discounts on a range of products and services including boat insurance, books, charts, DVD's and class certificates
- Access to expert advice on all aspects of boating from legal wrangles to training matters
- Free issue of Certificates of Competence, increasingly asked for by everyone from overseas governments to holiday companies, insurance underwriters to boat hirers

- Access to the wide range of RYA publications, including the quarterly magazine
- Third Party insurance for windsurfing members
- Free Internet access with RYA-Online
- Special discounts on AA membership
- Regular offers in RYA Magazine
- ...and much more

JOIN NOW

Membership form opposite or join online at *www.rya.org.uk*

Visit our website for information, advice, members' services and web shop.

1 Important

To help us comply with Data Protection legislation, please tick **either** Box A or Box B (you must tick Box A to ensure you receive the full benefits of RYA membership). The RYA will not pass your data to third parties.

☐ **A.** I wish to join the RYA and receive future information on member services, benefits and offers by post and email.

☐ **B.** I wish to join the RYA but do not wish to receive future information on member services, benefits and offers by post and email.

When completed, please send this form to: RYA, RYA House, Ensign Way, Hamble, Southampton, SO31 4YA

2

Title	Forename	Surname	Date of Birth			Male	Female
			D D / M M / Y Y				
1.			D D / M M / Y Y			☐	☐
2.			D D / M M / Y Y			☐	☐
3.			D D / M M / Y Y			☐	☐
4.			D D / M M / Y Y			☐	☐

Address

Town   **County**   **Post Code**

Evening Telephone   **Daytime Telephone**

email

Signature: _____   **Date:** _____

3 Type of membership required: *(Tick Box)*

☐ **Personal** *Annual rate £39 or £36 by Direct Debit*

☐ **Under 21** *Annual rate £13 (no reduction for Direct Debit)*

☐ **Family*** *Annual rate £58 or £55 by Direct Debit*

* Family Membership: 2 adults plus any under 21s all living at the same address

4 Please tick ONE box to show your main boating interest.

☐ Yacht Racing   ☐ Yacht Cruising
☐ Dinghy Racing   ☐ Dinghy Cruising
☐ Personal Watercraft   ☐ Inland Waterways
☐ Powerboat Racing   ☐ Windsurfing
☐ Motor Boating   ☐ Sportsboats and RIBs

Please see Direct Debit form overleaf

Instructions to your Bank or Building Society to pay by Direct Debit

Please complete this form and return it to:
Royal Yachting Association, RYA House, Ensign Way, Hamble, Southampton, Hampshire SO31 4YA

Originators Identification Number

9	5	5	2	1	3

5. To The Manager: Bank/Building Society

Address:

Post Code:

5. RYA Membership Number (For office use only)

2. Name(s) of account holder(s)

6. Instruction to pay your Bank or Building Society

Please pay Royal Yachting Association Direct Debits from the account detailed in this instruction subject to the safeguards assured by The Direct Debit Guarantee.

I understand that this instruction may remain with the Royal Yachting Association and, if so, details will be passed electronically to my Bank/Building Society.

3. Branch Sort Code

Signature(s) _____

Date _____

4. Bank or Building Society account number

Banks and Building Societies may not accept Direct Debit instructions for some types of account

Office use / Centre Stamp

Cash, Cheque, Postal Order enclosed   £

Made payable to the Royal Yachting Association

| **Office use only:** Membership Number Allocated |

077